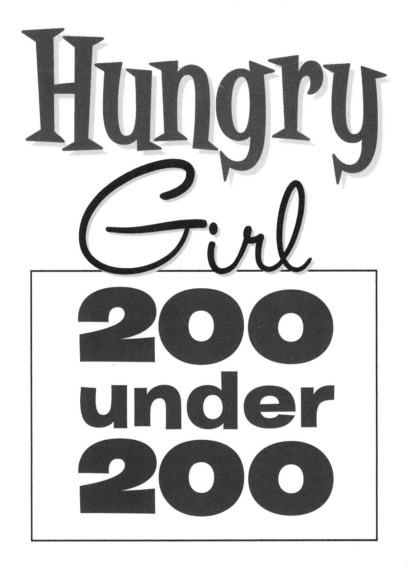

Hungry Girl

200 under 200

Also by Lisa Lillien

*Hungry Girl: Recipes and Survival Strategies
for Guilt-Free Eating in the Real World*

*Hungry Girl: The Official Survival Guides:
Tips & Tricks for Guilt-Free Eating*
(audio book)

Hungry Girl

200 under 200

200 Recipes Under 200 Calories

Lisa Lillien

St. Martin's Griffin
New York

HUNGRY GIRL: 200 UNDER 200: 200 RECIPES UNDER 200 CALORIES. Copyright © 2009 by Hungry Girl, Inc. All rights reserved. Printed in the United States of America. For information, address St. Martin's Press, 175 Fifth Avenue, New York, N.Y. 10010.

www.stmartins.com

Cover design and book design by Elizabeth Hodson

Illustrations by Jack Pullan

Food styling and photography by General Mills Photography Studios

     Photographer: Chuck Nields

     Food Stylists: Nancy Johnson and Sharon Harding

     Art Director: Chris Everett

ISBN-13: 978-0-312-55617-4

ISBN-10: 0-312-55617-9

10 9 8 7 6 5 4 3

This book is dedicated to my superhuman husband, Daniel Schneider, and to my wonderful parents, Florence and Maurice Lillien.
I love you all.

Contents

Acknowledgments

Thank you 1,000 times over to all the people who worked incredibly hard helping put this book together:

Elizabeth Hodson—you've been with HG every step (and bite) of the way. You help make everything we put out look amazingly adorable (and taste great!). **Jamie Goldberg**—your devotion and commitment to Hungry Girl (and guilt-free foods) is limitless. Your attention to detail: staggering. I'd say you're my right arm, but I'm a lefty. Saying thank you doesn't begin to express my deep appreciation for you both. **Lynn Bettencourt**—I am so thankful for those countless hours in the kitchen, at the office, and behind the camera. To **Lisa Friedman**—thank you for managing the book tours, and for your impeccable organization skills. **Dana DeRuyck**—thanks to you for your creativity, chewing, testing, cooking, and researching. To **Jennifer Curtis**—you live too far away, but we feel like you're always there with us. Thank you for your dedication and for all you do.

More thank yous . . .

Alison Kreuch—thank you for handling anything and everything I throw your way. If the U.S. could harness your energy, we wouldn't need foreign oil.

Super-agent **Neeti Madan**—you are the best agent ever. Hands down. Thank you.

To **Matthew Shear** and **Jennifer Enderlin**—thank you for continuing to believe in Hungry Girl (and for the extra color pages!). **John Karle**—thank you for putting up with me and for taking (most of) my calls. Thank you, as well, to **Anne Marie Tallberg**, **John Murphy**, and to all the rest of my friends over at St. Martin's Press.

Tom Fineman—thank you for your constant support, advice, and friendship. **Jeff Becker**—thank you for your guidance and for being such an active *Hungry Boy* (keep the emails coming). **John Vaccaro**—thank you for EVERYTHING always!

Special thanks also to **Debbie Puente**, **Jack Pullan**, and **Lisa Foiles**. And big thanks to the wonderful General Mills photography crew, as well as **David Witt**, **Greg Zimprich**, **Shelly Dvorak**, and **Dan Stangler**.

Thanks also to **Meri Lillien**, **Jay Lillien**, and to the fantastic **Lillien** and **Schneider families**.

To my furry babies, **Cookie** and **Jackson**, who are a constant source of happiness and comfort—much love!

And to my 700,000+ friends, the devoted Hungry Girl subscribers—THANK YOU, THANK YOU, THANK YOU!!!!!

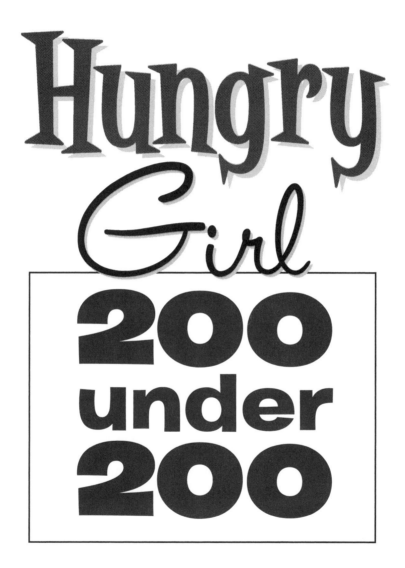

FAQs

Who/What is Hungry Girl?

Hungry Girl is a free daily email subscription service about guilt-free eating. The emails (which are read by over three-quarters of a million people a day) are packed with news, food finds, recipes, and real-world survival strategies. Hungry Girl was started by me, Lisa Lillien. I'm not a doctor or nutrition professional, I'm just hungry. And back in 2004, I decided I wanted to share my love and knowledge of food with the world, so Hungry Girl was born. To sign up for the daily emails or to see what you've missed since the beginning, go to Hungry-Girl.com.

The Hungry Girl philosophy is more of a lifestyle than anything else. There's no magic bullet or weight-loss secret that will make you lose and maintain weight. It's about finding a fun and satisfying way of eating you can live with forever.

Why 200 under 200? What is the significance of 200 calories?

Eating a lot of mini meals and snacks throughout the day is a great way to help you feel satiated, get that metabolism going, and keep you from ever becoming TOO ravenous (when that happens you're more likely to reach for the wrong foods and/or overeat). And if these mini meals contain around 200 calories, you can mix and match a whole bunch of them, or you can just incorporate a few into your diet, in a way that fits your daily life. While I do turn to snack bars on occasion, I would MUCH rather eat a small, satisfying meal or snack than a bar. And I think a lot of people feel the same way. This book is PACKED with recipes for delicious snacks, desserts, drinks, mini meals, and more that all have fewer than 200 calories. Keep in mind, this book is NOT meant to encourage people to drastically cut calories. In fact, I hope it helps you fill your diet with foods you love and achieve your weight-management goals, whether you're losing or maintaining.

How many calories should someone eat in a day?

That is an excellent question but one that I really can't answer. That number depends on many factors—your age, weight, height, gender, activity level, etc. To find out how many calories you should eat in a day, consult with your doctor or a nutrition professional.

What are HG recipes all about?

When it comes to HG recipes, the goal is to make them taste FANTASTIC—but also to keep them low in fat and calories. We also aim for high fiber counts, because fiber is great for you and helps keep you feeling full. Even though these recipes focus on keeping calorie and fat counts down, nutritional info is also provided for carbs, sugars, protein, etc., so you can look at a recipe and decide if it works for you.

What happens if I make substitutions for ingredients in some recipes?

Feel free to make substitutions for products and ingredients, but the taste and nutritional info will vary accordingly—so keep that in mind when swapping.

Where can I find Weight Watchers *POINTS*® values for the recipes in this book?

Here at HG, we love Weight Watchers. The plans are healthy and easy to follow, and they can fit a variety of lifestyles. That's why we feature *POINTS*® values in our daily emails and co-developed a bunch of recipes with Weight Watchers for this book. For a listing of *POINTS*® values for all the recipes in the book, go to hungry-girl.com/book.

Where can I find photos of all of the recipes in this book?

You can find beauteous color photos of every recipe in this book online at hungry-girl.com/book. And there are sixteen pages of color photos in the book, too.

Do you have a list of recommended products?

Yes. In fact, they are on the very next page! Yay . . .

Hungry Girl's Recommended Products

While the recipes in the book work well with many different products, we definitely have our favorites as far as taste and nutritional information are concerned. And we LOVE to name names. Here are some of our recommendations:

Light Soymilk (Vanilla, Chocolate, or Plain)
8th Continent Light Soymilk
Silk Light Soymilk
Blue Diamond Almond Breeze Unsweetened (technically not soymilk, but it's SO good and much lower in calories!)

Fat-Free Cheese
Kraft Fat Free Cheese
Lifetime Fat Free Cheese

Reduced-Fat Cheese
Sargento Reduced Fat Cheese
Kraft Reduced Fat Cheese Made with 2% Milk
Weight Watchers Reduced Fat Cheese

Fat-Free Cream Cheese
Philadelphia Fat Free Cream Cheese (in a tub, not in block-form)

Light Whipped Butter or Light Buttery Spread
Brummel & Brown
Land O'Lakes Whipped Light Butter
Smart Balance 37% Light Buttery Spread

Fat-Free Liquid Egg Substitute
Egg Beaters Original
Better 'n Eggs
Nulaid ReddiEgg

Fat-Free Yogurt
Yoplait Light Yogurt
Weight Watchers Yogurt
Dannon Light & Fit Nonfat Yogurt
Fiber One Creamy Nonfat Yogurt

Fat-Free Greek Yogurt
Fage Total 0% Greek Yogurt

Fat-Free Ice Cream
Breyers Double Churn FREE Fat Free Ice Cream
Dreyer's/Edy's Slow Churned Light Ice Cream (not completely fat-free, but it's AWESOME and will barely affect recipe nutritional info)

Whole-Wheat (or High-Fiber) Pitas
Weight Watchers 100% Whole Wheat Pita Pocket
Western Bagel The Alternative Pita Bread

Light English Muffins
Weight Watchers English Muffins
Thomas' Light Multi-Grain English Muffins
Thomas' 100 Calorie Original English Muffins
Western Bagel Alternative English Muffins

Boneless Skinless Lean Chicken Breast
Tyson Boneless, Skinless Chicken Breasts
Perdue Fit & Easy Boneless, Skinless Chicken Breasts

Frozen Ground-Beef-Style Soy Crumbles
Boca Meatless Ground Crumbles or Ground Burger
Morningstar Farms Meal Starters Grillers Recipe Crumbles

Extra-Lean Ground Turkey
Jennie-O Extra Lean Ground Turkey Breast
Butterball Extra Lean Ground Turkey Breast

98% Fat-Free Turkey Breast Slices
Oscar Mayer Oven Roasted Turkey Breast
Applegate Farms Smoked or Roasted Turkey Breast
Sara Lee Oven Roasted Turkey Breast

Turkey Pepperoni
Hormel Turkey Pepperoni

Soy Crisps or Mini Rice Cakes
Quaker Quakes Rice Snacks
Genisoy Soy Crisps

Freeze-Dried Fruit
Gerber Mini Fruits (found in the baby food aisle)
Crispy Green Crispy Fruit (crispygreen.com)
Just Tomatoes, ETC.! (justtomatoes.com)

Sugar-Free Pancake Syrup
Mrs. Butterworth's Sugar Free Syrup
Cary's Sugar Free Syrup
Log Cabin Sugar Free Syrup
Joseph's Sugar Free Syrup

No-Calorie Sweetener Packets
Splenda No Calorie Sweetener

Sugar-Free Syrup
Torani Sugar Free Syrup

Sugar-Free Powdered Drink Mix Packets
Crystal Light On The Go
Wyler's Light Singles to go!

25-Calorie Diet Hot Cocoa Packets
Swiss Miss Sensible Sweets Diet Hot Cocoa Mix

Nonstick Spray
Pam No-Stick Cooking Spray

Canned Brands We Love
Green Giant
S&W (low-calorie and low-sodium options)
Health Valley (fat-free, low-salt, and no-salt broth options)

Go-To Brand for Canned Pumpkin
Libby's

Go-To Brand for Oats and Oatmeal
Quaker

Go-To Brand for Frozen Veggies
Green Giant

Go-To Brand for Fresh Veggies and Broccoli Slaw Mix
Mann's Sunny Shores

Hungry Girl Staples

You'll find these specific products popping up in many of our recipes:

* Fiber One bran cereal (original)

* Splenda No Calorie Sweetener (granulated)

* Boca Original Meatless Burgers

* Bisquick Heart Smart baking mix

* Pillsbury Reduced Fat Crescent Rolls

* The Laughing Cow Light Original Swiss cheese

* La Tortilla Factory Smart & Delicious Low Carb/High Fiber Tortillas

* House Foods Tofu Shirataki, Fettuccine, and Spaghetti Shaped Noodle Substitute

* Cool Whip Free

* Fat Free Reddi-wip

* I Can't Believe It's Not Butter! Spray

* Coffee-mate Sugar Free French Vanilla powdered creamer

* Hellmann's/Best Foods Dijonnaise

* Frank's RedHot Original Cayenne Pepper Sauce

* Jell-O Sugar Free Pudding Snacks, assorted flavors

* chapter one

morning minis

Small A.M. Meals with Huge Appeal

Never skip breakfast. Everyone who tells you that—from your mom to your doctor—is 100 percent right. There's no reason to get all preachy and tell you WHY breakfast is so important . . . it just is. But huge breakfasts can bog you down and make you feel like a lazy slug. The light recipes in this chapter are creative, easy, fun, and EXTREMELY delicious. Wake up and eat, people!

fab-five banana pancake minis

PER SERVING (5 mini pancakes): 185 calories, 1g fat, 343mg sodium, 37g carbs, 5g fiber, 7.5g sugars, 9.5g protein

Yep, there are FIVE of these banana-licious babies in this single-serving recipe. And they have just the right amount of banana flavor. These are great with sugar-free pancake syrup or just a squirt of Fat Free Reddi-wip.

Ingredients

¼ cup whole-wheat flour
¼ cup mashed ripe banana (about half a banana's worth)
3 tablespoons fat-free liquid egg substitute
1 tablespoon light vanilla soymilk
¼ teaspoon baking powder
⅛ teaspoon vanilla extract
1 no-calorie sweetener packet
Dash salt
Dash cinnamon

Directions

In a small bowl, combine all dry ingredients (flour, baking powder, sweetener, salt, and cinnamon) until mixed well.

In a separate bowl, combine mashed banana with all wet ingredients (egg substitute, soymilk, and vanilla extract) until mixed thoroughly.

Combine dry and wet ingredients, and stir thoroughly.

Bring a large pan sprayed with nonstick spray to medium heat. Pour batter in the pan to form five mini pancakes. Once pancakes begin to look solid, after about 1 minute, gently flip.

Cook for an additional minute, or until both sides are lightly browned and insides are cooked through. Then plate 'em up and enjoy!

MAKES 1 SERVING

complete & utter oatmeal insanity

PER SERVING (entire recipe): 179 calories, 3.5g fat, 367mg sodium, 40g carbs, 11g fiber, 3g sugars, 7g protein

Yes, the idea of tossing SO many things (including whipped cream) into oatmeal may in fact be a little insane. But we wouldn't have it any other way! This is one of my very favorite decadent breakfasts.

Ingredients

1 packet plain instant oatmeal
¼ cup Fiber One bran cereal (original)
¼ cup light vanilla soymilk
2 tablespoons canned pure pumpkin
2 tablespoons Fat Free Reddi-wip
1 tablespoon sugar-free pancake syrup
¼ teaspoon pumpkin pie spice
5 sprays I Can't Believe It's Not Butter! Spray
1 no-calorie sweetener packet
Dash salt

Directions

Place all ingredients except for Reddi-wip in a medium microwave-safe bowl. Add ¼ cup water and stir.

Microwave for 45 seconds, then mix well.

Microwave for an additional 30 to 40 seconds. Allow oatmeal to thicken before removing from the microwave.

Add Reddi-wip and stir well. Then enjoy the best bowl of oatmeal you've EVER tasted!

MAKES 1 SERVING

Chew on This

The city of Lafayette, Colorado, REALLY loves oatmeal! Each January the city hosts an oatmeal festival, featuring a bake-off, health screenings, a big hearty 'n healthy oatmeal breakfast, and (sometimes) an oatmeal mini spa!

spinach, tomato, feta 'n egg wrap attack

PER SERVING (entire wrap): 168 calories, 5.5g fat, 694mg sodium, 24g carbs, 15g fiber, 2g sugars, 20g protein

This was conjured up when the folks at Starbucks threatened to pull the plug on their version of this popular breakfast wrap. They decided not to (yay!), but that was after our version was already whipped up (double yay!).

Ingredients

1 large La Tortilla Factory Smart & Delicious Low Carb/High Fiber tortilla
½ cup chopped fresh spinach
⅓ cup fat-free liquid egg substitute
1½ tablespoons crumbled reduced-fat feta cheese with basil and tomato flavoring (plain is fine, too)
1 tablespoon canned fire-roasted diced tomatoes with garlic
2 pieces sun-dried tomato packed in oil and spices, chopped

Directions

Spray a small pan with nonstick spray and bring to medium heat. Add egg substitute and cook to form an egg patty, flipping and folding until firm, about 1 to 2 minutes on each side. Remove egg patty and set aside.

Remove pan from heat, re-spray, and then return to medium heat. Add chopped spinach and both types of tomatoes. Cook for about 1 minute, stirring occasionally, until spinach has wilted.

Add cheese to the pan and cook for an additional 30 seconds, until softened. Remove from heat and allow to cool slightly.

Meanwhile, heat tortilla in the microwave until slightly warm. Place veggie-cheese mixture in the center of the tortilla. Place egg patty on top and wrap the tortilla up envelope style, folding the sides in first and then rolling it up from the bottom.

Place wrap in the toaster oven, seam side down, and bake for 1 to 2 minutes, until thoroughly heated. Enjoy!

MAKES 1 SERVING

HG Fast Fact:

The original Starbucks wrap has 240 calories, 10 grams fat, and 7 grams fiber. Not bad, especially for the 'Bucks! However, as you can see, there's always room for improvement.

slammin' smoked salmon 'n bacon b-fast sandwich

PER SERVING (entire sandwich): 194 calories, 3g fat, 936mg sodium, 25g carbs, 6g fiber, 2g sugars, 19.5g protein

OMG! This little sandwich is CRAZY-decadent. The combo of smoked salmon, turkey bacon, and red onion mixed with cream cheese is so good, you may actually cry when you taste it. Not exaggerating here, people!

◌ Ingredients

1 light English muffin
1 ounce smoked salmon, roughly chopped
1 slice extra-lean turkey bacon
2 tablespoons fat-free cream cheese
1 tablespoon chopped red onion
1 tablespoon chopped cucumber
1 slice tomato

◌ Directions

Cook bacon slice according to package directions, either in the microwave or in a pan sprayed with nonstick spray. Once cool enough to handle, chop the bacon into small pieces.

In a small dish, combine cream cheese with smoked salmon, chopped bacon, onion, and cucumber until mixed well.

Split muffin into halves, and heat or toast halves.

Spread cream cheese mixture over half of the English muffin. Top with the tomato slice.

Finish it all off with the other muffin half, pressing down firmly. Your sandwich is now ready for consumption!

MAKES 1 SERVING

 For a pic of this recipe, see the first photo insert. Yay!

tutti frutti biscuits

PER SERVING (1 biscuit): 132 calories, 2.25g fat, 240mg sodium, 26g carbs, 2g fiber, 7.5g sugars, 3.5g protein

These biscuits are INCREDIBLE. They're not overly sweet, and they have a bit of a scone-like feel to them but with the softer texture of a biscuit.

Ingredients

⅔ cup canned bite-sized fruit cocktail packed in juice, drained well

⅔ cup regular oats (not instant)

⅓ cup Bisquick Heart Smart baking mix

¼ cup light vanilla soymilk

2 tablespoons sugar-free strawberry preserves

1 tablespoon Splenda No Calorie Sweetener (granulated)

1 tablespoon brown sugar (not packed)

2 teaspoons light whipped butter or light buttery spread, melted and cooled

¾ teaspoon baking powder

Dash salt

Directions

Preheat oven to 425 degrees.

In a small bowl, mix preserves with a fork until a syrup-like consistency is reached. Pat fruit cocktail as dry as possible, eliminating as much moisture as you can. Toss fruit cocktail in the preserves until thoroughly coated. Set aside.

In a medium bowl, combine oats, baking mix, Splenda, brown sugar, baking powder, and salt. Stir in melted butter and mix well.

Add soymilk and stir until mixed thoroughly. Then fold fruit mixture into the batter.

On a baking sheet sprayed with nonstick spray, divide batter into 4 evenly spaced mounds. Bake for about 12 minutes, or until tops are firm and edges begin to brown. Let cool slightly, and then enjoy!

MAKES 4 SERVINGS

 For a pic of this recipe, see the first photo insert. Yay!

Chew on This

The lyrics to Little Richard's hit song are "Tutti Frutti, all rooty." "All rooty" was hipster slang at the time for "all right." No, the song isn't about someone named Rudy. . .

creamy hot apple b-fast with brown sugar crunch

Hot breakfast in a bowl is awesome, but so many people complain that they're bored with it. Be a little kooky! This recipe calls for a granola bar, apples, and a few other key ingredients. It's PERFECT for a chilly fall or winter morning.

Ingredients

1 cup peeled apple chunks (any sweet, not tart, variety)
1 Nature Valley Maple Brown Sugar Crunchy Granola Bar (half a 2-bar package)
1½ teaspoons sugar-free fat-free vanilla instant pudding mix
2 no-calorie sweetener packets
1½ teaspoons cornstarch
½ teaspoon cinnamon
Dash salt

Directions

In a medium-large microwave-safe bowl, place pudding mix, sweetener, cornstarch, cinnamon, and salt. Add ⅓ cup cold water and stir until blended.

Add apple chunks to the bowl and toss them in the liquid mixture. Cover bowl and microwave for 2½ minutes. Allow mixture to thicken and cool for a few minutes before removing from the microwave.

Meanwhile, place the granola bar in a sealable plastic bag. Place on a flat surface, and use a rolling pin or a can to crush the bar through the bag until you have small crumbly pieces.

Once bowl containing apple mixture is cool enough to handle, stir in granola pieces. Devour immediately!

MAKES 1 SERVING

Chew on This

The first McIntosh apples were discovered on a mutated apple tree in Canada. Luckily, John McIntosh was an adventurous eater. Mmmmm, what delicious mutant apples you have!

choco-monkey oatmeal

PER SERVING (entire recipe): 185 calories, 2g fat, 137mg sodium, 37g carbs, 5g fiber, 11g sugars, 6.5g protein

This recipe is NOT recommended for monkeys, although they would probably love it (they're not stupid!). Chocolate-banana oatmeal is a yummy treat for all humans (kids especially love this stuff).

Ingredients

⅓ cup regular oats (not instant)
One 25-calorie packet diet hot cocoa mix
One-half medium banana, mashed
⅛ teaspoon cinnamon
1 no-calorie sweetener packet
Dash salt

Directions

Pour cocoa mix into a glass with cinnamon, sweetener, and salt. Add ¼ cup hot water and stir thoroughly. Once cocoa mix has dissolved, add ¼ cup cold water and stir.

In a large microwave-safe cereal bowl, combine cocoa mixture with mashed banana and oats until mixed well. Microwave for 2 minutes.

Give it a stir, and then allow oatmeal to cool and thicken. Enjoy!

MAKES 1 SERVING

Chew on This

Ever wonder if monkeys TRULY like bananas or if it's just a myth? Well, it's absolutely true. Thing is, monkeys like pretty much all fruit, and it just so happens that bananas and monkeys are native to similar regions. So be a good monkey and eat your fruit!

grab 'n go breakfast cookies

PER SERVING (1 cookie): 154 calories, 1.5g fat, 166mg sodium, 32.5g carbs, 5g fiber, 10.5g sugars, 5g protein

These breakfast cookies are such a hit, we're constantly whipping up batches to keep around the HG HQ for snacking. And if you make 'em in the P.M. you'll have super-quick b-fasts for the next few A.M.s! They're slightly addictive, though, so watch out!

○ Ingredients

½ cup regular oats (not instant)
6 tablespoons whole-wheat flour
¼ cup Fiber One bran cereal (original)
¼ cup Splenda No Calorie Sweetener (granulated)
⅓ cup Gerber peaches (or another brand of pureed peaches found in the baby food aisle)
¼ cup canned pure pumpkin
¼ cup fat-free liquid egg substitute
1 tablespoon golden raisins
1 tablespoon Ocean Spray Craisins (original)
2 tablespoons brown sugar (not packed)
2 teaspoons Coffee-mate Sugar Free French Vanilla powdered creamer
½ teaspoon baking powder
½ teaspoon cinnamon
⅛ teaspoon salt

○ Directions

Preheat oven to 375 degrees.

Chop raisins and Craisins into small pieces. Set aside.

In a food processor or blender, grind Fiber One to a breadcrumb-like consistency.

In a large bowl, combine oats, flour, Fiber One crumbs, Splenda, brown sugar, baking powder, cinnamon, and salt until mixed well.

In a medium bowl, dissolve powdered creamer in 2 tablespoons hot water. Add all other wet ingredients (pureed peaches, pumpkin, and egg substitute) and stir until mixed well.

Add liquid mixture to dry ingredients and stir until completely blended. Slowly sprinkle chopped raisins and Craisins into the batter, making sure they don't all stick together.

Spray a large baking sheet with nonstick spray and spoon batter into 4 evenly spaced circles. Spread batter out a bit with the back of a spoon.

Bake in the oven for 12 to 14 minutes, until tops of treats are just slightly crispy. Allow to cool slightly on the sheet. Grab 'n go!

MAKES 4 SERVINGS

📷 For a pic of this recipe, see the first photo insert. Yay!

For Weight Watchers **POINTS**® values and photos of all the recipes in this book, check out hungry-girl.com/book.

eggless stuffed breakfast burrito

PER SERVING (entire burrito): 199 calories, 6g fat, 892mg sodium, 28g carbs, 15g fiber, 5.5g sugars, 21g protein

Who says breakfast burritos NEED some sort of egg? Is there a rule? This burrito has cheese, veggies, and bacon—and it is completely egg-free. Weeeeee!

Ingredients

1 large La Tortilla Factory Smart & Delicious Low Carb/High Fiber tortilla
1 slice extra-lean turkey bacon
2 cups fresh spinach leaves
⅓ cup diced mushrooms
¼ cup diced plum tomatoes (preferably Roma)
¼ cup diced green bell pepper
2 tablespoons diced onion
1 wedge The Laughing Cow Light Original Swiss cheese
2 tablespoons shredded fat-free cheddar cheese

Directions

Cut bacon into small, bite-sized pieces. Set aside.

Spray a small pan with nonstick spray and bring to medium-high heat. Add bacon pieces, mushrooms, pepper, and onion to the pan. Stirring occasionally, cook until bacon begins to crisp, 4 to 5 minutes.

Add spinach leaves and cook and stir until the leaves have wilted. Add shredded cheese and stir until just melted. Remove pan from heat and set aside.

Warm tortilla in the microwave for about 10 seconds. Lay tortilla flat and spread cheese wedge on top of it. Evenly layer spinach mixture over the cheese—topped tortilla. Place diced tomatoes on top of spinach mixture.

Fold in the sides of the tortilla, and then carefully roll tortilla up from the bottom to the top. Enjoy!

MAKES 1 SERVING

cinnamon-vanilla french toast nuggets

PER SERVING (8 nuggets): 151 calories, 2.25g fat, 299mg sodium, 24g carbs, 1.5g fiber, 3.5g sugars, 8.5g protein

Yes, we made French toast out of hot dog buns. Don't judge us. These are actually AWESOME and fluffy. And you get to eat EIGHT nuggets. That rocks!

Ingredients

2 hot dog buns
⅓ cup fat-free liquid egg substitute
1 teaspoon Coffee-mate Sugar Free French Vanilla powdered creamer
2 dashes cinnamon
Optional topping: sugar-free pancake syrup

Directions

Split each bun in half and cut each of those halves into 4 pieces, leaving you with 16 chunks of bread.

In a small bowl, dissolve powdered creamer in 1 tablespoon warm water. Add egg substitute and 1 dash cinnamon, stirring until mixed well.

Bring a large pan sprayed with nonstick spray to medium-high heat. Dip or soak bread pieces in egg mixture, covering them completely. Place egg-dipped bread pieces in the pan and cook for 3 to 5 minutes, flipping occasionally to cook all sides.

Remove from heat and plate your nuggets. Sprinkle with another dash cinnamon. If you like, top with some sugar-free pancake syrup.

MAKES 2 SERVINGS

Chew on This

Most of us know it as "French toast," but in France they actually call the dish *"pain perdu,"* which means "lost bread." The theory is that even if you forget about your bread and it gets a little stale, you can soften it up by dunking it in egg. Genius!

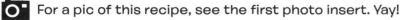 For a pic of this recipe, see the first photo insert. Yay!

cheesy-good breakfast tartlets

PER SERVING (2 tartlets): 111 calories, 2g fat, 553mg sodium, 10.5g carbs, 0.5g fiber, 1.5g sugars, 11g protein

These are overflowing with cheesed-up egg, turkey bacon, and more. They're a little fancy, so feel free to serve them to brunch guests. No one (except you) will know they're low in calories and fat. NO ONE.

Ingredients

1 cup fat-free liquid egg substitute
8 small square wonton wrappers
2 slices extra-lean turkey bacon
1 cup chopped mushrooms
⅓ cup chopped scallions
1 wedge The Laughing Cow Light Original Swiss cheese, room temperature
2 tablespoons fat-free cream cheese, room temperature
48 sprays I Can't Believe It's Not Butter! Spray
¼ teaspoon sea salt
Optional: additional salt, black pepper

Directions

Preheat oven to 350 degrees.

Spray 8 cups of a 12-cup muffin pan with nonstick spray and set aside.

On a clean, dry surface, spread out wonton wrappers. Spray each one with 3 sprays of butter, and use your fingers to spread butter evenly over each wrapper. Gently flip wrappers and repeat on the other sides.

Carefully transfer wonton wrappers to the muffin pan, placing each wrapper in a muffin cup and pressing it in to form the cup shape. Bake in the oven for 10 minutes, until wonton cups are firm and brown.

Prepare bacon slices according to package directions, either in the microwave or in a pan sprayed with nonstick spray. Once cool enough to handle, chop the bacon into small pieces and set aside.

In a small bowl, combine egg substitute and salt and whisk until blended. Stir in the scallions. Set aside.

In a small microwave-safe dish, combine cheese wedge and cream cheese. Stir until blended. Warm in the microwave for 15 seconds, and then stir again. Set aside.

Bring a medium pan sprayed with nonstick spray to medium heat on the stove. Add mushrooms, and cook and stir for 2 minutes.

Add egg mixture to the pan. Scramble as you would ordinary eggs. Once solid bits begin to form, slowly fold in cheese mixture, one spoonful at a time. Continue to cook and stir until egg mixture is solid.

Remove from heat and mix chopped bacon into the pan immediately. Evenly distribute egg mixture among the baked wonton cups. Serve warm. If you like, season to taste with a little salt and/or black pepper. Yum!

MAKES 4 SERVINGS

📷 For a pic of this recipe, see the first photo insert. Yay!

For Weight Watchers **POINTS**® values and photos of all the recipes in this book, check out hungry-girl.com/book.

creamy crunchy freeze-dried frenzy

PER SERVING (entire recipe): 165 calories, 0.5g fat, 180mg sodium, 40g carbs, 7g fiber, 12g sugars, 11g protein

Okay, this so-called frenzy is actually a parfait. But the word "frenzy" makes it seem a little more exciting, no? Freeze-dried fruit and Fiber One cereal make this breakfast super-crunchy.

⊙ Ingredients

6 ounces fat-free vanilla yogurt
¼ cup freeze-dried fruit (any variety)
¼ cup Fiber One bran cereal (original)

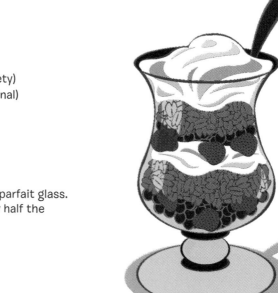

⊙ Directions

Place half the yogurt in a bowl or parfait glass. Top with half the fruit followed by half the cereal. Repeat.

Now devour!

MAKES 1 SERVING

HG Tip! This recipe can be made with any type of freeze-dried fruit, so pick your favorite. We like to grab Gerber's Mini Fruits blend of banana and strawberries from the baby food aisle. And even though the package warns, "This product should only be fed to a seated and supervised child," we eat 'em anyway . . . and we're not always seated and supervised.

berries & cream oatmeal pudding

PER SERVING (entire recipe): 190 calories, 2.5g fat, 501mg sodium, 35.5g carbs, 5g fiber, 7g sugars, 5.5g protein

Gotta be honest . . . This isn't always the prettiest breakfast on the table, but it tastes FANTASTIC. So ignore the scary array of colors that emerge from your bowl and dig in. Mmmmmmmm!

Ingredients

⅓ cup regular oats (not instant)
½ cup frozen unsweetened mixed berries
¼ cup light vanilla soymilk
1 tablespoon sugar-free fat-free vanilla instant pudding mix
1 teaspoon Coffee-mate Sugar Free French Vanilla powdered creamer
1 no-calorie sweetener packet
Dash salt

Directions

In a medium microwave-safe bowl, combine powdered creamer with ¼ cup warm water. Stir until dissolved.

Add soymilk and pudding mix, and stir until mixture is thoroughly blended. Add all of the other ingredients to the bowl and stir.

Microwave for 3 minutes. Allow to cool and thicken. Dig in!

MAKES 1 SERVING

For Weight Watchers *POINTS*® values and photos of all the recipes in this book, check out hungry-girl.com/book.

big fat blueberry muffins

PER SERVING (1 muffin): 137 calories, 2.25g fat, 269mg sodium, 26.5g carbs, 3g fiber, 7.5g sugars, 4g protein

These muffins are phenomenal. Plain and simple. And while they ARE big and fat, they're NOT fattening.

Ingredients

1 cup whole-wheat flour
1 cup fresh blueberries
½ cup light vanilla soymilk
¼ cup sugar-free pancake syrup
¼ cup fat-free liquid egg substitute
¼ cup Splenda No Calorie Sweetener (granulated)
3 tablespoons brown sugar (not packed)
2 tablespoons light whipped butter or light buttery spread, room temperature
2 tablespoons no-sugar-added applesauce (get Mott's Blueberry Delight if you can find it!)
1½ teaspoons baking powder
½ teaspoon vanilla extract
¼ teaspoon salt

Directions

Preheat oven to 400 degrees.

In a medium mixing bowl, combine flour, Splenda, brown sugar, baking powder, and salt, stirring until mixed well.

In a large mixing bowl, combine soymilk, syrup, egg substitute, butter, applesauce, and vanilla extract. Using an electric mixer or a whisk, mix until thoroughly blended. Do not worry if butter bits do not break up completely.

Add dry ingredients in the first mixing bowl to wet ingredients in the large mixing bowl and mix until completely blended. Then fold in blueberries.

Line a 6-cup muffin pan (or half a 12-cup pan) with baking liners and/or spray with nonstick spray. Evenly distribute batter among the 6 cups.

Bake in the oven for about 22 minutes, until a toothpick inserted into the center of a muffin comes out clean. Enjoy!

MAKES 6 SERVINGS

Chew on This

SHOCKER ALERT! Besides berries, a Starbucks blueberry muffin is stuffed with around 500 calories and 19 grams fat. Ahhhhhhh!

easy caprese breakfast pizzas

This is HG's latest way to have pizza for breakfast. Fresh basil is soooo good!

Ingredients

1 light English muffin
2 thick slices from a large firm plum tomato (we recommend Roma)
6 fresh basil leaves
1 piece light mozzarella string cheese, pulled into strips
1 teaspoon light whipped butter or light buttery spread
½ teaspoon crushed garlic
Optional: salt, black pepper

Directions

Preheat oven to 375 degrees.

In a small dish, combine butter and garlic. Mix well and set aside.

Bring a pan sprayed with nonstick spray to medium-high heat on the stove. Cook tomato slices for 1 to 2 minutes on each side, until lightly blackened.

Split English muffin into halves. Spread garlic-butter mixture evenly over both halves. Top each half evenly with mozzarella cheese strips.

Place three basil leaves on top of each cheese-topped muffin half, followed by tomato slices.

Place halves on a baking sheet sprayed lightly with nonstick spray. Bake in the oven until the cheese has melted and muffin halves are toasty, about 5 minutes.

Finish off with a dash of salt and pepper on top of each tomato, if you like. Then devour!

MAKES 1 SERVING

 For a pic of this recipe, see the first photo insert. Yay!

HG Fast Fact:

Caprese means "in the style of Capri," an island off the coast of Italy (about halfway down the west side of the boot). The colors in the traditional salad of tomato, basil, and mozzarella are a tribute to the Italian flag. A DELICIOUS tribute.

For Weight Watchers *POINTS*® values and photos of all the recipes in this book, check out hungry-girl.com/book.

oat-rageous chocolate chip pancake minis

PER SERVING (5 mini pancakes): 179 calories, 3.25g fat, 341mg sodium, 28g carbs, 3.5g fiber, 5g sugars, 9.5g protein

These chocolate chip pancakes have fewer than 40 calories each. And even though they're "mini," they pack in a tremendous amount of chocolate flavor.

Ingredients

3 tablespoons regular oats (not instant)
3 tablespoons fat-free liquid egg substitute
2 tablespoons whole-wheat flour
1 tablespoon light vanilla soymilk
½ tablespoon mini semi-sweet chocolate chips
¼ teaspoon baking powder
⅛ teaspoon vanilla extract
1 no-calorie sweetener packet
Dash salt

Directions

Place all ingredients in a small bowl, except for chocolate chips. Add 1 tablespoon water and stir until thoroughly mixed. Fold in chocolate chips.

Bring a large pan sprayed with nonstick spray to medium heat. Pour batter in the pan to form 5 mini pancakes. Once pancakes begin to look solid, after about 1 minute, gently flip.

Cook for an additional minute, or until both sides are lightly browned and insides are cooked through. Plate 'em and commence chewing!

MAKES 1 SERVING

Chew on This

How's this for inventive? Ruth Graves Wakefield of the Toll House Inn decided she wanted to put pieces of chocolate in her cookies, and that's just what she did. She chopped up a Nestlé chocolate bar, and mixed in the bits. The result was so good that she told Nestlé, "Hey! Why don't you make little bits of chocolate so I can put them in my cookies?" (Okay, maybe those weren't her exact words, but you get the picture.)

piña colada parfait surprise

PER SERVING (entire parfait): 175 calories, 0.5g fat, 129mg sodium, 42g carbs, 5g fiber, 28g sugars, 8g protein

This tropical morning treat will make you feel like you're on vacation. And (SURPRISE!), it's got bananas in it, too!

Ingredients

6 ounces fat-free vanilla yogurt
¼ cup canned pineapple tidbits packed in juice, drained
¼ cup chopped banana
2 tablespoons Fiber One bran cereal (original)
¼ teaspoon coconut extract

Directions

Mix coconut extract into yogurt. Place about one-third of the yogurt mixture in the bottom of a parfait glass, or any small glass.

Top with half of the pineapple tidbits and half of the chopped banana.

Sprinkle half of the cereal over the fruit layer, and then spoon another third of the yogurt on top.

Add remaining pineapple and banana, and then add a final layer of yogurt.

Finish it all off with the rest of the cereal. Enjoy!

MAKES 1 SERVING

For a pic of this recipe, see the first photo insert. Yay!

Chew on This

The earliest known reference to a piña colada appeared in an article in *Travel* magazine in 1922. One key ingredient wasn't originally there—the coconut! "Piña colada" translates literally to "strained pineapple." Some creative mixologist threw the coconut in much later. Very interesting . . .

sweet cinna-muffin

PER SERVING (entire recipe): 126 calories, 3.25g fat, 268mg sodium, 22g carbs, 6g fiber, <0.5g sugars, 6g protein

This is a PERFECT little breakfast treat or anytime snack.
It's buttery, sweet, and cinnamony. Yum!

Ingredients

1 light English muffin
1 teaspoon light whipped butter or light buttery spread
10 sprays I Can't Believe It's Not Butter! Spray
¾ teaspoon Splenda No Calorie Sweetener (granulated)
¼ teaspoon cinnamon

Directions

Split English muffin in half, and then spread each half evenly with butter spread.

In a small dish, combine Splenda and cinnamon until mixed well. Sprinkle Splenda-cinnamon mixture over muffin halves.

Spray each muffin half with 5 sprays of butter spray. Heat in the microwave (for a soft Cinna-Muffin) or in the toaster oven (for a crunchy Cinna-Muffin). Consume immediately. Weeeeee!

MAKES 1 SERVING

Chew on This

Cinnamon is one of the oldest known spices. Because it was sought by early explorers, some people say that cinnamon contributed to the discovery of America. A stretch? Perhaps.

peachy maple–caramel crunch parfait

PER SERVING (entire parfait): 174 calories, 0.5g fat, 212mg sodium, 37.5g carbs, 1.5g fiber, 26.5g sugars, 8.5g protein

Here's another breakfast parfait recipe for you. This one combines the flavors of peach, caramel, and maple. Hence the name.

Ingredients

6 ounces fat-free vanilla yogurt
½ cup chopped peaches
4 caramel soy crisps or mini rice cakes, crushed
2 tablespoons sugar-free pancake syrup
Dash cinnamon

Directions

Stir pancake syrup into yogurt and set aside.

Place a third of the peaches in the bottom of a parfait glass, or any small glass. Add half of the yogurt.

Top with another third of the peaches. Cover with half of the caramel crunchies.

Spoon the rest of the yogurt on top, and cover with remaining fruit and crunchies. Sprinkle with cinnamon and enjoy!

MAKES 1 SERVING

For Weight Watchers **POINTS**®
values and photos of all the
recipes in this book, check out
hungry-girl.com/book.

fro-yo'ed up oatmeal sundae

PER SERVING (entire sundae): 198 calories, 4.25g fat,
219mg sodium, 38g carbs, 4g fiber, 11.5g sugars, 5.5g protein

We like to be creative when it comes to breakfast, and this recipe is particularly
fun. We put together a tasty bowl of fruity oatmeal and then snazzed
it up with some frozen yogurt. Fro-yo for breakfast. Yee-ha!

Ingredients

¼ cup quick-cooking oatmeal

¼ cup low-fat vanilla frozen yogurt

¼ cup fresh blueberries

¼ cup sliced fresh strawberries

1 tablespoon strawberry (or any fruit flavor) sugar-free preserves

½ tablespoon All Natural Almond Accents in Original Oven Roasted or Honey Roasted

1 no-calorie sweetener packet

⅛ teaspoon cinnamon

Dash salt

HG Heads Up!
Irish oatmeal is
soooo good in this
recipe! It's heartier
and more filling than
regular oatmeal.

Directions

In a microwave-safe bowl, combine
oatmeal with ½ cup water. Microwave for
1 to 2 minutes, until desired consistency
is reached.

Once bowl of oatmeal is cool enough
to handle, mix in preserves, sweetener,
cinnamon, and salt. Top with fruit.

Place frozen yogurt on top of fruit layer, and then sprinkle with almonds.

Serve immediately—the frozen yogurt will melt, but it's delicious as it melts into the oatmeal!

MAKES 1 SERVING

 For a pic of this recipe, see the first photo insert. Yay!

HG Fast Fact:

In the classic holiday movie *Frosty the Snowman*, one of the children suggests that they name their snowman Oatmeal. Sounds pretty appropriate now, considering this chilly oatmeal breakfast. . .

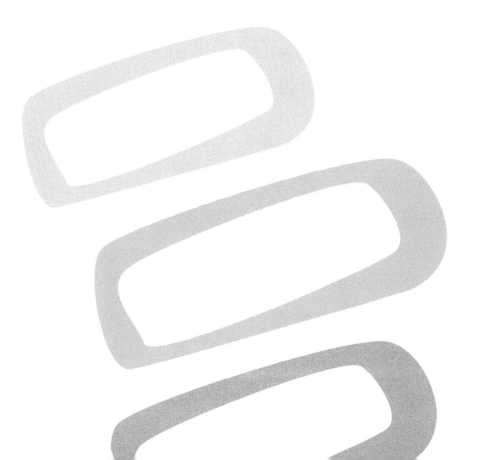

gooey cinnamon rolls with cream cheese icing

PER SERVING (1 iced roll): 126 calories, 5g fat, 308mg sodium, 18.5g carbs, <0.5g fiber, 6.5g sugars, 3g protein

Honestly, this is one of those recipes that's so good, it'll either make you laugh hysterically or cry uncontrollably. Emotion will ooze from you when you bite into one of these. Try it and see. You'll never think about eating a Cinnabon again.

Ingredients

HG Heads Up!
These cinnamon rolls double as breakfast AND dessert!

For Dough
1 package Pillsbury Reduced Fat Crescent Rolls refrigerated dough
16 sprays I Can't Believe It's Not Butter! Spray

For Filling
¼ cup dark brown sugar (not packed)
¼ cup Splenda No Calorie Sweetener (granulated)
½ tablespoon light whipped butter or light buttery spread, room temperature
1½ teaspoons cinnamon
⅛ teaspoon salt

For Icing
¼ cup Cool Whip Free, thawed
3 tablespoons fat-free cream cheese, room temperature
1 tablespoon Splenda No Calorie Sweetener (granulated)

Directions

Preheat oven to 375 degrees.

To make filling, combine all ingredients in a medium bowl, stirring well to make sure the butter gets mixed in evenly. Set aside.

To make icing, combine all ingredients in a small bowl and mix until smooth and blended. Place in the fridge to chill and set.

Prepare a dry surface by sprinkling it with a small amount of flour to prevent sticking. Remove dough from package and knead into a ball.

Using a rolling pin dusted lightly with flour, very firmly roll out dough into a thin sheet about 8 inches by 12 inches. Spray the dough's surface evenly with butter.

Spread filling out evenly over dough, leaving a ½-inch border around the edges.

Starting with a long side of the dough, roll it up tightly, forming a log. Once dough is completely rolled up, pinch the long seam to seal.

Turn the log over so that the seam is facing down. Using a very sharp knife, cut log into 8 even pieces, being careful not to squish dough.

Spray a baking pan with nonstick spray and arrange pieces of dough in the pan with swirl sides facing up. Use your hands to firmly press down on the tops of the pieces. Pinch the side seams to seal, if necessary.

Cover pan with aluminum foil. Bake in the oven for 8 minutes.

Remove foil and return pan to oven. Bake for an additional 5 minutes, or until cinnamon rolls have risen and are slightly browned on top.

Evenly distribute icing over cinnamon rolls and then enjoy!

MAKES 8 SERVINGS

 For a pic of this recipe, see the first photo insert. Yay!

chapter two

Egg-stravaganza

Omelettes, Scrambles, Frittatas, and More

I love egg whites and Egg Beaters so much it's scary. Really. Not a day goes by here at the HG HQ that we don't eat concoctions featuring some sort of low-calorie egg item—scrambled or baked with veggies, low-fat cheeses, and other stuff. This chapter contains a slew of recipes that are each great to enjoy as part of a meal or as a stand-alone snack.

Egg-cellent!

the breakfast club

PER SERVING (entire recipe): 195 calories, 2g fat, 663mg sodium, 6g carbs, 1g fiber, 4g sugars, 36g protein

With turkey, bacon, and tomato, it's like a club sandwich on your breakfast plate! Only you get to enjoy it without the risk of biting into a toothpick. Try topping it with a little ketchup, salt, and pepper.

Ingredients

⅔ cup fat-free liquid egg substitute
2 ounces raw extra-lean ground turkey
2 slices extra-lean turkey bacon
½ cup chopped tomatoes
Optional toppings: ketchup, hot sauce, salt, pepper, etc.

Directions

Cook bacon according to package directions, either in a pan with nonstick spray or in the microwave. Once cool enough to handle, chop the bacon into bite-sized pieces. Set aside.

Bring a pan sprayed with nonstick spray to medium heat. Add ground turkey and use a spatula to break it up and crumble it as it cooks. Once turkey is no longer pink, about 2 minutes, add egg substitute to the pan. Scramble until mostly solid.

Add bacon pieces and continue to cook until the scramble is fluffy and fully cooked. Plate it up and top with the chopped tomatoes. If you like, finish it off with your favorite egg-friendly add-ons. Happy breakfasting!

MAKES 1 SERVING

HG Trivia Tidbit:

In the movie *The Breakfast Club*, Ally Sheedy's character eats a Cap'n Crunch and Pixy Stix sandwich. FYI, this sandwich is NOT Hungry Girl approved.

frittata italiano

PER SERVING (¼th of recipe): 82 calories, 1.5g fat, 310mg sodium, 5g carbs, 1.25g fiber, 2.5g sugars, 12g protein

This delicious frittata was co-developed with our pals over at The Double W. You'll enjoy its classic Italian flavor... Yum!

This recipe was co-developed with Weight Watchers®.

Ingredients

4 cups fresh spinach, chopped
4 medium plum tomatoes (preferably Roma), chopped
1½ cups fat-free liquid egg substitute
2 tablespoons grated Parmesan cheese
¼ teaspoon Italian seasoning, or more to taste
Dash salt

Directions

Preheat broiler.

Spray a large oven-safe pan with nonstick spray. Bring to medium heat on the stove. Add spinach and tomatoes. Cook and stir until spinach has wilted, about 1½ minutes. Sprinkle with salt.

In a small bowl, whip egg substitute with Italian seasoning. Pour into the pan and cook until edges of frittata are almost set, tilting pan as necessary, about 3 minutes.

Sprinkle with Parmesan cheese and place pan under broiler. Broil until fully cooked, 3 to 4 minutes. Slice into four pieces and serve.

MAKES 4 SERVINGS

HG Tip! If you're not sure if the handle of your pan is oven-safe, wrap it with aluminum foil.

ginormous oven-baked omelette

PER SERVING (¼th of recipe): 140 calories, 3g fat, 387mg sodium, 9g carbs, 1g fiber, 5g sugars, 18g protein

This omelette lives up to its name. It really IS ginormous. Bake this at night, and then nuke it in the A.M. for a fluffy, hot egg breakfast that's ready in seconds. It's even good cold. (Shhhhh ... don't tell anyone HG told you that!)

Ingredients

2 cups fat-free liquid egg substitute
½ cup fat-free milk
½ cup reduced-fat shredded cheese (any flavor)
1 cup sliced bell peppers (any color)
1 cup sliced mushrooms
½ cup sliced tomatoes
½ cup sliced onions
1 tablespoon reduced-fat Parmesan-style grated topping
¾ teaspoon garlic powder
⅛ teaspoon black pepper
Optional toppings: ketchup, salsa, hot sauce

Directions

Preheat oven to 375 degrees.

Spray a deep, round casserole dish (about 9 inches wide) with nonstick spray. Pour egg substitute and milk into the dish. Add shredded cheese, tomatoes, garlic powder, and black pepper, and stir until mixed well. Set aside.

Bring a large pan sprayed with nonstick spray to high heat on the stove. Sauté peppers, onions, and mushrooms for about 2 minutes, stirring occasionally, just long enough to brown the outsides of the vegetables. Add the veggie mixture to the casserole dish and mix well.

Bake in the oven for 30 minutes. Carefully remove the dish from the oven, and evenly cover with Parm-style grated topping.

Return dish to the oven and bake for 20 to 25 minutes, until the top has puffed and the omelette is firm.

Allow to cool slightly before serving, then cut into four slices. Finish with the optional ingredients, if you like, or any of your favorite omelette toppers!

MAKES 4 SERVINGS

Chew on This

The longest distance an uncooked egg has been thrown successfully **WITHOUT BREAKING** is 323 feet, 2 inches, according to *The Guinness World Records*. Think of the ginormous (but dirty) omelette that could have been made with all the eggs that **BROKE!**

For Weight Watchers *POINTS*®
values and photos of all the
recipes in this book, check out
hungry-girl.com/book.

that's a lotta frittata

PER SERVING (¼th of recipe): 120 calories, 2.5g fat, 469mg sodium, 9.5g carbs, 2g fiber, 3.5g sugars, 14.5g protein

A lotta veggies... a lotta flavor... a lotta frittata! This thing is very large and extremely delicious.

◻ Ingredients

4 cups chopped arugula

1½ cups fat-free liquid egg substitute

1 cup chopped red bell pepper

1 cup chopped summer squash (like zucchini or yellow squash)

½ cup shredded reduced-fat mozzarella cheese

½ cup canned sweet corn, drained

1 teaspoon minced garlic

¼ teaspoon salt

Optional: additional salt, black pepper, cayenne pepper

◻ Directions

Preheat broiler.

In a medium bowl, whisk egg substitute and salt. Set aside.

Spray a large oven-safe pan with nonstick spray. Bring to medium heat on the stove. Add garlic and cook for 1 minute.

Add arugula to the pan, and cook and stir until wilted, 1 to 2 minutes. Remove arugula mixture from pan and set aside.

Remove pan from heat and re-spray with nonstick spray. Return pan to medium heat on the stove. Place bell pepper and squash in the pan. Cook for 3 minutes, stirring occasionally. Add corn and continue to cook for another 2 minutes. Return arugula to the pan, stir, and arrange the veggie mixture so that it covers the bottom of the pan evenly.

Pour egg mixture over veggies, and tilt pan back and forth to ensure egg substitute is evenly distributed. If needed, run a spatula along the sides of the pan to help egg to flow underneath veggies. Cook for 2 minutes, and then remove pan from heat.

Sprinkle mozzarella cheese evenly on top of the frittata. Place pan under the broiler for 2 to 4 minutes, until the egg starts to puff up and the mixture is set.

Allow to cool, then cut into four slices. Season to taste with optional ingredients, if you like. Chew!

MAKES 4 SERVINGS

For a pic of this recipe, see the first photo insert. Yay!

HG Tip! If you're not sure whether the handle of your pan is oven-safe, wrap it with aluminum foil.

cheesed-up pepperoni pizza scramble

PER SERVING (entire scramble): 173 calories, 2.5g fat, 1,226mg sodium, 7.5g carbs, 0.5g fiber, 3g sugars, 27g protein

We are pizza-obsessed over here in HG land. This dish actually tastes like REAL pepperoni pizza, only in scrambled form.

○ Ingredients

½ cup fat-free liquid egg substitute
⅓ cup shredded fat-free mozzarella cheese
¼ cup canned diced tomatoes with Italian seasonings, drained
9 slices turkey pepperoni, quartered
Dash salt
Dash oregano
Dash garlic powder
Optional: black pepper

○ Directions

Bring a pan sprayed with nonstick spray to medium heat. Add egg substitute and turkey pepperoni, and scramble as you would ordinary eggs. Add salt, oregano, garlic powder and, if you like, black pepper.

Once scramble begins to look solid, after about 1 minute, add tomatoes. Scramble for another 30 seconds or so.

Sprinkle with mozzarella, reduce heat to low, and cover pan. Let cook for another 30 seconds, until cheese has melted and—voilà—you're done!

MAKES 1 SERVING

 For a pic of this recipe, see the first photo insert. Yay!

HG Trivia Tidbit:

Cold pizza is a surprisingly popular breakfast food, and not just among college students. One *ABC News* poll cited that 39 percent of Americans have, at some point, eaten cold pizza for breakfast. We much prefer this pizzalicious scramble.

mexi-licious smothered taco scramble

PER SERVING (entire scramble): 168 calories, 1g fat, 1,154mg sodium, 11.5g carbs, 2g fiber, 3.5g sugars, 27.5g protein

Hey! It's a Mexican fiesta in the form of a scramble. Spicy, zesty, creamy, cheesy ... Olé!

Ingredients

½ cup fat-free liquid egg substitute
¼ cup frozen ground-beef-style soy crumbles, thawed
¼ cup shredded fat-free cheddar cheese
1 teaspoon dry taco seasoning mix
3 tablespoons salsa
1 tablespoon fat-free sour cream

Directions

Bring a pan sprayed with nonstick spray to medium heat. Add egg substitute and sprinkle with taco seasoning. Scramble until solid bits begin to form. Next add soy crumbles and scramble until fully cooked.

Remove from heat and transfer to a microwave-safe plate. Sprinkle with cheese and microwave for 25 to 30 seconds, until cheese has melted. Smother with salsa and sour cream.

MAKES 1 SERVING

HG Fast Fact:

Wondering what kind of spices go into taco seasoning? McCormick Taco Seasoning Mix has chili pepper, cumin, oregano, red pepper, onion, salt, sugar, paprika, and garlic. So, if you want to try to make your own, have fun!

hula scramble

PER SERVING (entire scramble): 186 calories, 3.5g fat, 1,117mg sodium, 11.5g carbs, 0.5g fiber, 8.5g sugars, 24.5g protein

Eating this scramble is like taking a Hawaiian vacation right in your very own kitchen. Okay, maybe it's not EXACTLY like that, but it is a vacation from boring old run-of-the-mill egg dishes.

Ingredients

½ cup fat-free liquid egg substitute

2 ounces (about 4 slices) thinly sliced extra-lean ham, chopped

1 canned pineapple ring packed in juice, chopped

1 wedge The Laughing Cow Light Original Swiss cheese, cut into pieces

Directions

Bring a pan sprayed with nonstick spray to medium heat. Add ham and pineapple. Cook for 2 minutes, stirring occasionally.

Add egg substitute and scramble with the ham and pineapple. Once scramble is a little more than halfway cooked, add cheese pieces. Continue to scramble until cheese has melted and egg substitute is fully cooked. Eat up!

MAKES 1 SERVING

Chew on This

The pineapple is neither a pine nor an apple. Discuss! Alright, here's something else . . . Pineapple juice can be used as both a marinade and a meat tenderizer. Cool!

hakuna frittata

PER SERVING (⅛th of recipe): 84 calories, 2g fat, 446mg sodium, 6g carbs, 1.5g fiber, 1.5g sugars, 10.5g protein

Spinach + mushrooms + artichokes = Hakuna. We made that up. Let's see if it sticks.

Ingredients

6 cups fresh spinach leaves, chopped

1½ cups fat-free liquid egg substitute

1½ cups sliced portabello mushrooms

1 cup canned artichoke hearts packed in water, drained very well and chopped

½ cup shredded reduced-fat cheddar cheese

2 tablespoons finely chopped shallots

1 teaspoon minced garlic

¼ teaspoon salt

Optional: additional salt, black pepper, cayenne pepper

Directions

Preheat broiler.

Whisk egg substitute and salt in a medium bowl for about 1 minute. Set aside.

Bring a large oven-safe pan sprayed with nonstick spray to medium heat on the stove. Add garlic and shallots, and cook for 1 minute.

Add spinach to pan. Cook and stir until wilted, 1 to 2 minutes. Remove veggie mixture from pan and set aside.

Remove pan from heat, and re-spray with nonstick spray. Return pan to heat, and add mushrooms and artichoke hearts. Cook for about 3 minutes, stirring occasionally until veggies start to soften.

Chew on This

Artichokes aren't just veggies—they're actually flower buds. If they blossom, they produce a violet blue flower 7 inches across. Beauteous!

Return spinach mixture to the pan, mix well, and then spread the contents of the pan out so they cover the bottom of the pan evenly.

Pour egg mixture over veggies, and tilt pan back and forth to ensure egg substitute is evenly distributed. If needed, run a spatula along the sides of the pan to help egg to flow underneath veggies. Cook for 2 minutes, and then remove from heat.

Sprinkle cheese evenly on top of the frittata. Place pan under the broiler for 2 to 3 minutes, until the egg starts to puff up and mixture is set.

Allow to cool, and then cut into six pieces. Season to taste with optional spices, if you like.

MAKES 6 SERVINGS

HG Tip! If you're not sure if the handle of your pan is oven-safe, wrap it with aluminum foil.

For Weight Watchers *POINTS*®
values and photos of all the
recipes in this book, check out
hungry-girl.com/book.

"it's all greek to me" scramble

PER SERVING (entire scramble): 152 calories, 4.5g fat,
665mg sodium, 9g carbs, 1.5g fiber, 4.5g sugars, 19.5g protein

Oooooh, it's like a little Greek salad—in breakfast form! Mmmmmmm . . .

Ingredients

½ cup fat-free liquid egg substitute
¼ cup crumbled reduced-fat feta cheese
6 grape tomatoes, halved
2 tablespoons chopped red onion
Basil, garlic powder, black pepper, to taste

Directions

Bring a pan sprayed with nonstick spray to medium heat. Add onion and tomatoes, and cook, stirring occasionally, until onion is slightly browned, about 2 minutes.

Add egg substitute and scramble for 2 to 3 minutes, until fully cooked.

Plate your scramble and top with crumbled feta. Season to taste with basil, garlic powder, and pepper. Chew.

MAKES 1 SERVING

meaty 'n manly breakfast toastie

PER SERVING (entire recipe): 196 calories, 3.75g fat,
925mg sodium, 17g carbs, 8g fiber, 1.5g sugars, 29g protein

Here's an unconventional one: This is sort of a breakfast tostada loaded
with various meats and topped with sour cream. You'll love it—and so will
all the boys (and men) in your life...

Ingredients

1 original (not large) La Tortilla Factory Smart & Delicious Low Carb/High Fiber tortilla
½ cup fat-free liquid egg substitute
1 slice extra-lean turkey bacon
1 slice extra-lean ham, cut into small pieces
¼ cup frozen ground-beef-style soy crumbles, thawed
1 tablespoon fat-free sour cream
Salt and black pepper, to taste

Directions

Prepare bacon slice according to package directions, either in the microwave or in a pan
sprayed with nonstick spray. Once cool enough to handle, chop the bacon into small pieces.
Set aside.

Bring a small pan sprayed with nonstick spray to medium heat. Pour in egg substitute, then
add bacon, soy crumbles, and ham. Scramble until fully cooked, about 2 minutes.

Meanwhile toast your tortilla in a toaster oven until crispy. Top tortilla with your meaty
scramble. Season to taste with salt and pepper. Finish it all off with sour cream. Eat daintily
with a knife and fork, or pick it up and eat it like a man! Grrrrrrrr . . .

MAKES 1 SERVING

el ginormo oven-baked southwest omelette

PER SERVING (¼th of recipe): 188 calories, 3g fat, 590mg sodium, 17g carbs, 2.5g fiber, 5g sugars, 22g protein

El Ginormo, directly translated, means "The Ginormo." And "The Ginormo" translates to mean "large, Mexican-inspired egg meal infused with bell pepper, chilies, beans, and more." Yayayayay!!!

Ingredients

2½ cups fat-free liquid egg substitute

½ cup fat-free milk

½ cup shredded reduced-fat cheese blend (look for one with cheddar and Monterey Jack)

½ cup chopped red bell pepper

½ cup chopped onion

½ cup canned black beans, rinsed and drained

½ cup canned sweet corn, drained

¼ cup canned diced green chilies

1 tablespoon minced garlic

1 teaspoon cumin

½ teaspoon dry taco seasoning mix

Optional toppings: salsa, fat-free sour cream, chopped scallions

Directions

Preheat oven to 375 degrees.

Line a deep, round casserole dish (about 9 inches wide) with aluminum foil. Spray lightly with nonstick spray, making sure to coat the sides as well as the bottom.

In a large bowl, combine egg substitute, milk, cumin, and taco seasoning. Whisk mixture for 1 minute, until mixed thoroughly.

Add all of the other ingredients and mix well. Carefully transfer egg mixture to the casserole dish.

Bake in the oven for 60 to 70 minutes, until the top has puffed and the center is firm. Allow to cool slightly before cutting.

Cut into four slices. If you like, finish off with the optional toppings—we highly recommend 'em!

MAKES 4 SERVINGS

HG Fast Fact:

Research shows that black beans are just as high in antioxidants as fruity powerhouses like grapes and cranberries. Maybe that's why beans are called the "magical fruit." (Okay, maybe not.)

super-cheesy
all-american breakfast bake

PER SERVING (entire recipe): 159 calories, 2.5g fat,
972mg sodium, 7g carbs, 1.25g fiber, 3g sugars, 24g protein

This is a fun little breakfast to serve if you're having guests over because it
SEEMS like it's fancy and fattening, but it's simple and totally low in calories.
Just remember to make one for each person. It's too good to share!

Ingredients

2 cups fresh spinach leaves
½ cup fat-free liquid egg substitute
1 wedge The Laughing Cow Light Original Swiss cheese
1 slice fat-free American cheese
1 slice extra-lean turkey bacon
Salt and black pepper, to taste

Directions

Preheat oven to 375 degrees.

Cook bacon according to
package instructions, either in
the microwave or in a pan with
nonstick spray. Once cool enough
to handle, chop the bacon into
small pieces.

Bring a pan sprayed with nonstick spray to medium heat on the stove. Add spinach, and
cook and stir until wilted.

Spray a small, round baking dish (5 to 6 inches wide) with nonstick spray. Place spinach
in the dish. Break cheese wedge into quarters and place on top of spinach. Cover with
bacon pieces.

Pour egg substitute over bacon, and top with slice of American cheese. Bake for 20 to 25 minutes, until egg substitute is firm and fully cooked. Season to taste with salt and pepper, and then enjoy!

MAKES 1 SERVING

 For a pic of this recipe, see the first photo insert. Yay!

Chew on This

Calling something "cheesy" used to be a compliment, meaning that it was a big deal. Eventually, slang and sarcasm got a hold of the term, twisted it around, and it came to mean the exact opposite. In our defense, this bake is "cheesy" in the old-school way.

For Weight Watchers *POINTS*® values and photos of all the recipes in this book, check out hungry-girl.com/book.

turkey 'n swiss scramble

PER SERVING (entire scramble with sauce): 191 calories, 5.25g fat, 1,189mg sodium, 10.5g carbs, 0.5g fiber, 5.5g sugars, 23.5g protein

If you like turkey and Swiss sandwiches, this scramble will make you very happy. We're all about getting creative with egg-based breakfasts!

Ingredients

For Scramble
½ cup fat-free liquid egg substitute
1½ ounces (about 3 slices) 98 percent fat-free turkey breast slices
1 slice reduced-fat Swiss cheese
2 slices tomato

For Sauce
1 tablespoon fat-free mayonnaise
1 teaspoon Dijonnaise
1 teaspoon light whipped butter or light buttery spread

Directions

To make the sauce, combine mayo, Dijonnaise, and butter in a small microwave-safe dish. Mix well, and then set aside.

Chop the turkey and cheese into bite-sized pieces, and set aside.

Bring a pan sprayed with nonstick spray to medium-high heat. Grill the tomato slices for about 2 minutes on each side. Set aside.

Remove pan from heat, and lightly re-spray with nonstick spray. Return pan to medium-high heat.

Pour egg substitute into pan, and cover with turkey and cheese bits. Scramble until fully cooked, 2 to 3 minutes. Remove from heat and plate your scramble.

Heat sauce for about 20 seconds in the microwave. Once heated, stir in 2 teaspoons warm water.

Place the tomato slices on top of the scramble, and then smother the whole dish with sauce.

MAKES 1 SERVING

HG Trivia Tidbit:

Americans are on the turkey bandwagon, BIG TIME! Since 1970, the amount of turkey eaten in the U.S. has gone up 116 percent, totaling around 17.5 pounds per person each year. (29 percent of it gets gobbled down over the holidays!) Good news for us, bad news for turkeys . . .

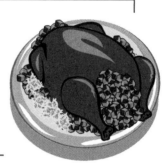

snazzy spanish omelette

PER SERVING (entire omelette with sauce): 191 calories, <0.5g fat,
1,120mg sodium, 27g carbs, 4g fiber, 7g sugars, 19g protein

This recipe is AWESOME, people. It may take a few minutes longer to prepare than some of our other scrambles and omelettes, but it's definitely worth it!

Ingredients

For Omelette
⅔ cup fat-free liquid egg substitute
½ cup peeled and thinly sliced potatoes
2 tablespoons diced onion
⅛ teaspoon salt
Pinch baking powder

For Sauce
¼ cup canned tomato sauce
¼ cup diced green bell pepper
2 tablespoons diced onion
2 tablespoons canned fire-roasted diced tomatoes
1 tablespoon salsa
¼ teaspoon minced garlic

Directions

To make the sauce, bring a small pot sprayed with nonstick spray to medium-high heat. Add the onion, bell pepper, and garlic, and cook for 3 to 4 minutes, until browned.

Add tomato sauce, tomatoes, and salsa to the veggie mix, stirring to mix, then bring to a boil.

Once the sauce is boiling, reduce to a simmer. Stir and cook for 1 additional minute. Remove sauce from heat and set aside.

To make the omelette, place the potatoes and onion in a medium microwave-safe bowl. Add ¼ cup hot water. Cover bowl and microwave for about 5 minutes, until potatoes are nice and soft. Once bowl is cool enough to handle, drain excess water.

Mash the potato-onion mixture. Add the egg substitute, salt, and baking powder, and stir well.

Bring a medium pan sprayed with nonstick spray to medium-high heat. Gently pour in the potato-egg mixture. Cook until the bottom is firm, about 4 to 5 minutes.

Using a spatula, slide omelette onto a dinner plate. Carefully place pan over plate. Using potholders or kitchen towels, hold pan and plate firmly together. Flip both and return pan to the stove, with the omelette in the pan.

Continue to cook until the center of the omelette is completely cooked through, 3 to 4 minutes.

Plate the omelette and pour the sauce on top. *¡Buen apetito!*

MAKES 1 SERVING

HG Tip! Keep potholders or kitchen towels handy for this recipe. It involves some fancy flipping.

chapter three

scoopable salads

Deli Done Right

I am probably more proud of this chapter than any other in the book, simply because so-called scoopable deli salads are usually the most deceptively high-calorie items on restaurant menus. Hundreds of calories and dozens and dozens of fat grams typically hide in those mayo-packed concoctions. The recipes in this chapter cleverly use key ingredients in ways that ensure creaminess *and* deliciousness—yet they are all extremely low in calories and fat. Pile these on beds of lettuce, stuff 'em inside high-fiber tortillas, or eat them straight from the bowls you make 'em in.

redhot chick'n salad

PER SERVING (¾ cup): 142 calories, 2.25g fat, 585mg sodium, 6g carbs, 0.5g fiber, 2g sugars, 25g protein

This scoopable chicken salad was inspired by classic Buffalo wings. It's got the heat, the ranch, and even the celery and carrots. What it doesn't have is all the fat and calories. Yay!

Ingredients

6 ounces cooked skinless lean chicken breast, cubed

3 tablespoons fat-free mayonnaise

3 tablespoons chopped celery

3 tablespoons chopped carrots

2 teaspoons reduced-fat Parmesan-style grated topping

1½ teaspoons Frank's RedHot Original Cayenne Pepper Sauce

½ teaspoon dry ranch dip/dressing mix

Directions

In a medium bowl, combine mayo, Frank's, and ranch mix, and stir well.

Add chicken, celery, and carrots to the saucy mayo, and stir.

Sprinkle with Parm-style topping, and stir again.

Enough stirring . . . eat up!

MAKES 2 SERVINGS

For Weight Watchers **POINTS**® values and photos of all the recipes in this book, check out hungry-girl.com/book.

veggie-loaded tangy tuna salad

PER SERVING (about ¾ cup): 153 calories, 2.5g fat, 730mg sodium, 14g carbs, 2g fiber, 7g sugars, 18g protein

The problem with most tuna salads is that they rely on gobs of mayo for flavor. This one gets its deliciousness from relish, honey mustard, and a slew of veggies. Mmmmm!

Ingredients

One 6-ounce can tuna packed in water, drained and flaked
½ cup finely chopped sweet bell pepper (red, orange, yellow, or any combination)
¼ cup finely chopped carrots
¼ cup finely chopped celery
⅓ cup fat-free mayonnaise
2 teaspoons honey mustard
1 teaspoon sweet relish
Dash salt
Dash black pepper
Optional: additional salt and black pepper

Directions

In a medium bowl, combine mayo, honey mustard, relish, salt and black pepper. Mix well, then stir in tuna.

Fold in all of the veggies. Season to taste with more salt and black pepper, if you like. Mmmmmm!

MAKES 2 SERVINGS

 For a pic of this recipe, see the first photo insert. Yay!

citrus-licious egg white salad

PER SERVING (about 1 cup): 90 calories, 1g fat, 556mg sodium, 9g carbs, 1.5g fiber, 4g sugars, 11g protein

It's a little sweet, a little citrusy, and REALLY delicious. You will NOT miss the yolks at all. Promise!

Ingredients

6 large hard-boiled egg whites, chilled and chopped
¼ cup finely chopped celery
¼ cup finely chopped red bell pepper
¼ cup finely chopped red onion
3 tablespoons fat-free mayonnaise
1 teaspoon creamy Dijon mustard
1 teaspoon lime juice
½ teaspoon lemon juice
⅛ teaspoon salt
⅛ teaspoon black pepper

Directions

Place onion in a small microwave-safe bowl with 1 tablespoon water. Cover and microwave for 1½ minutes. Once bowl is cool enough to handle, drain water and allow the onion to cool completely.

In another small bowl, combine mayo, mustard, lime juice, lemon juice, salt, and black pepper, stirring until mixed well.

Once onion has cooled completely, add chopped egg whites, bell pepper, and celery, and stir. Then add mayo mixture, and stir until thoroughly mixed. Time to devour!

MAKES 2 SERVINGS

Chew on This

An average serving of egg salad has close to 400 calories and more than 30 grams of fat. THAT is completely unacceptable.

sweet 'n chunky chicken salad

PER SERVING (about 1 cup): 145 calories, 1.5g fat, 332mg sodium, 14g carbs, 1g fiber, 10g sugars, 21g protein

Grapes and apples add fruity fun to this one. The result is sweet, creamy chicken salad you'll FLIP over! Pssst . . . the short, sweet cucumbers called for in this recipe are great—but if you can't find 'em, any cucumber will do.

Ingredients

4½ ounces cooked skinless lean chicken breast, roughly chopped
½ cup chopped Persian or Kirby cucumber
⅓ cup red seedless grapes, halved
⅓ cup chopped apples
¼ cup plain fat-free yogurt
2 tablespoons fat-free mayonnaise
1 no-calorie sweetener packet
¼ teaspoon lemon-pepper seasoning
Dash salt

Directions

In a medium bowl, combine yogurt, mayo, sweetener, lemon-pepper seasoning, and salt, stirring until mixed well.

Add chicken, stirring until fully coated with the yogurt dressing.

Add cucumber, grape halves, and apples, and mix well. Try not to pass out as you chow down on this insanely good chicken salad!

MAKES 2 SERVINGS

 For a pic of this recipe, see the first photo insert. Yay!

go greek chicken salad

PER SERVING (about 1 cup): 173 calories, 2.75g fat, 474mg sodium,
7.5g carbs, 0.5g fiber, 4g sugars, 30g protein

This Greek-salad-inspired chicken creation is fantastic. The feta, yogurt,
and black olives work so well together, and the result is super-creamy. It's hard to
believe there are less than 3 grams of fat in a serving, but it's true!

Ingredients

6 ounces cooked skinless lean chicken breast, roughly chopped
½ cup chopped cucumber
⅓ cup cherry tomatoes, quartered
¼ cup crumbled fat-free feta cheese with Mediterranean herbs (plain will do if flavored
    is not available)
¼ cup plain fat-free yogurt
2 tablespoons fat-free mayonnaise
2 tablespoons canned sliced black olives
Optional: salt, black pepper, lemon juice

Directions

In a medium bowl, combine yogurt and mayo until mixed well.

Add remaining ingredients and stir until coated.

Add optional ingredients, to taste, if you like.

Once completely mixed, refrigerate for about 30 minutes. But if you can't wait that
long, it's okay to eat right away!

MAKES 2 SERVINGS

veggie-loaded tropical crab salad

PER SERVING (about 1 cup): 115 calories, 0.5g fat, 812mg sodium, 16g carbs, 1.5g fiber, 12g sugars, 10g protein

Make this salad with real crab or fake crab—either works well! It's sweet and tasty. The veggies give it a nice crunch, too.

Ingredients

One 6-ounce can lump crabmeat, rinsed and drained
½ cup finely chopped green cabbage
¼ cup diced red bell pepper
¼ cup diced sweet onion
¼ cup canned crushed pineapple in juice, lightly drained
¼ cup plain fat-free yogurt
2 tablespoons seasoned rice vinegar
One-half no-calorie sweetener packet
⅛ teaspoon paprika
⅛ teaspoon salt
Optional: additional paprika and salt, black pepper

Directions

In a microwave-safe bowl, toss cabbage, red bell pepper, and onion with vinegar. Cover and microwave for 2 minutes. Uncover and refrigerate until cool, about 30 minutes.

Meanwhile, in a separate bowl, combine yogurt, sweetener, paprika, and salt. Stir in the crab and pineapple, and refrigerate until the veggies have cooled.

Combine contents of both bowls and mix well. Refrigerate until completely chilled. Season to taste with optional ingredients, if you like. Enjoy!

MAKES 2 SERVINGS

HG Trivia Tidbit:

When someone is being a grouch, quite often we'll call that person "crabby." The root of the word comes from the old English "crabba," meaning "to scratch or claw." (Yup, that sounds like a crab.) This salad, on the other hand, may sweeten up even the crabbiest of humans!

spicy taco tuna salad

PER SERVING (½ cup): 111 calories, 1.5g fat, 663mg sodium, 6g carbs, 1g fiber, 3g sugars, 17.5g protein

If you're not crazy about spicy foods, just leave out the cayenne pepper. And if you're just crazy, add more of it!

⊃ Ingredients

One 6-ounce can tuna packed in water, drained and flaked
2 tablespoons fat-free mayonnaise
2 tablespoons salsa
2 tablespoons chopped red bell pepper
2 tablespoons chopped green bell pepper
1 tablespoon chopped onion
1 tablespoon taco sauce
¾ teaspoon dry taco seasoning mix
½ teaspoon chili powder
¼ teaspoon cayenne pepper

⊃ Directions

In a medium bowl, combine mayo, salsa, taco sauce, taco seasoning mix, chili powder, and cayenne pepper until mixed thoroughly.

Add the tuna, bell peppers, and onion into sauce mixture, and stir. Refrigerate for 30 minutes before eating.

MAKES 2 SERVINGS

For Weight Watchers *POINTS*®
values and photos of all the
recipes in this book, check out
hungry-girl.com/book.

i can't believe it's not potato salad!

PER SERVING (⅔ cup): 97 calories, 1.25g fat, 729mg sodium, 17g carbs, 3g fiber, 8g sugars, 4.5g protein

This salad tastes so much like the real thing, we DARE you to try it out on friends. DON'T tell anyone it's made with cauliflower—they'll think they're eating creamy potato salad. DO IT! Come on, you've been dared. P.S. This stuff tastes even better the day after it's prepared.

Ingredients

1 large head cauliflower, roughly chopped
6 hard-boiled egg whites, chilled and chopped
½ envelope dry ranch dressing/dip mix
1½ cups fat-free mayonnaise
½ cup fat-free sour cream
3 tablespoons Hellmann's/Best Foods Dijonnaise
2 tablespoons fat-free non-dairy liquid creamer
1 cup diced red onion
2 celery stalks, diced
¼ cup chopped chives
3 tablespoons seasoned rice vinegar
2 tablespoons chopped dill
2 tablespoons chopped parsley
¼ teaspoon salt
Optional garnish: paprika

Directions

Place cauliflower in a large microwave-safe bowl, and pour ⅓ cup water over it. Cover and microwave for 6 to 8 minutes, until cauliflower is soft.

Meanwhile, in a medium bowl, stir together ranch mix, mayo, sour cream, Dijonnaise, and salt. Set aside.

Once bowl is cool enough to handle, drain any excess water from cauliflower. Lightly mash 2 cups of the cauliflower (set the rest aside), and then place mashed cauliflower in a blender. Add creamer and puree or pulse until blended. Don't worry if the puree isn't completely smooth. Pour mayo mixture into the blender, and mix until blended and creamy.

Chop remaining cauliflower into small, ½-inch pieces. Place cauliflower in a large bowl, and add onion, celery, and vinegar. Toss well and let sit for 5 minutes.

Pour blender mixture over the vegetables and mix well. Add chopped egg whites, chives, dill, and parsley. Stir lightly.

Chill for several hours before serving. Sprinkle with paprika, if you like. Mmmmm!

MAKES 10 SERVINGS

 For a pic of this recipe, see the first photo insert. Yay!

Backyard BBQ Newsflash!
Your average potato salad contains nearly 30 grams of fat per cup. THAT is insulting to potatoes.

every day is thanksgiving salad

PER SERVING (about ¾ cup): 117 calories, 1g fat, 270mg sodium, 10g carbs, 1g fiber, 6g sugars, 17.5g protein

This is a brilliant little turkey salad that tastes EXACTLY like Thanksgiving. No need to wait 'til November, though! Just whip up a batch anytime. By the way, it's even good cold—just like most Thanksgiving leftovers!

Ingredients

4½ ounces cooked skinless lean turkey breast, chopped
⅓ cup chopped celery
¼ cup fat-free chicken or turkey gravy
2 tablespoons chopped onion
2 tablespoons Ocean Spray Craisins (original)
Dash salt
Dash black pepper
Dash thyme
Optional: additional salt, black pepper, and thyme

Directions

In a medium microwave-safe dish, combine turkey and gravy. Heat for about 30 seconds in the microwave.

Stir in all of the other ingredients and mix well. Season to taste with optional ingredients, if you like. Eat!

MAKES 2 SERVINGS

coconut-glaze fruit salad

PER SERVING (1 cup): 122 calories, 1g fat, 20mg sodium,
28.5g carbs, 3.5g fiber, 20.5g sugars, 2.5g protein

WOW. This tropical fruit salad is sooooo super-delicious, you will
absolutely *desert fatty desserts* when it's around.

Ingredients

For Salad
2 cups halved strawberries
1 cup blueberries
1 cup red grapes
1 cup chopped peaches
1 large banana, sliced
1 large apple, chopped
Optional: fresh mint leaves

For Glaze
6 ounces fat-free vanilla yogurt
¼ cup light coconut milk
2 tablespoons Splenda No Calorie Sweetener (granulated)
¼ teaspoon coconut extract
¼ teaspoon lime juice

Directions

In a large bowl, combine all of the fruit. Set aside.

In a mixing bowl, combine all glaze ingredients until mixed well.

Add glaze to fruit bowl. Toss to coat all fruit evenly. Mix in some mint leaves, if you like.
Refrigerate until ready to serve!

MAKES 6 SERVINGS

creamy crab salad

PER SERVING (about ¾ cup): 112 calories, 1.75g fat,
776mg sodium, 11.5g carbs, 0.5g fiber, 5g sugars, 12.5g protein

Creamy... crunchy... crabby (in a good way). This salad tastes like
it is LOADED with calories and fat—but all it has is great,
creamy seafood taste (and lots of crunchy veggies!).

Ingredients

Two 6-ounce cans lump crabmeat, rinsed and drained
½ cup fat-free sour cream
½ cup fat-free mayonnaise
¼ cup plus 1 tablespoon fat-free cream cheese, room temperature
½ cup chopped celery
¼ cup finely chopped sweet or yellow onion
¼ cup thinly sliced scallions
¼ cup chopped red bell pepper
⅛ teaspoon cayenne pepper
Optional: salt and black pepper

Directions

In a pan sprayed with nonstick spray, cook onion
over high heat for about 1 minute, until browned.
Remove from heat and set aside.

In a medium bowl, combine sour cream, mayonnaise,
and cream cheese. Whisk until smooth. Add browned onion, celery, scallions, bell pepper,
and cayenne pepper, stirring until mixed well. Gently stir in crabmeat.

Refrigerate for at least 1 hour to allow flavors to combine. Season to taste with salt and
black pepper, if you like.

MAKES 4 SERVINGS

scoopable chinese chicken salad

PER SERVING (1½ cups): 195 calories, 2.75g fat, 595mg sodium, 21g carbs, 4.5g fiber, 12.5g sugars, 22.5g protein

We took our sassy slaw recipe (see page 84 for that!) and turned it into a full-on mini meal. It is sooooooooooooooooo good!

Ingredients

One 16-ounce package dry broccoli slaw mix
12 ounces cooked skinless lean chicken breast, chopped
1 cup canned water chestnuts, drained and sliced into thin strips
1 cup canned mandarin orange segments packed in water or juice, drained and chopped (and rinsed, if packed in juice)
1 cup chopped scallions
¾ cup Newman's Own Lighten Up! Low Fat Sesame Ginger Dressing

Directions

In a large bowl, toss all ingredients together until mixed well.

Refrigerate for at least 2 hours. Stir well before serving. Enjoy!

MAKES 5 SERVINGS

 For a pic of this recipe, see the first photo insert. Yay!

chapter four

start
me up!

Appetizers, Sides, and Small Bites

Soups, muffins, a slaw, appetizers, sides . . . you'll find them all in this chapter. And boy are they gooooooood! The best part about these recipes is that they're so low in calories, you can combine 'em with ones from the mini meal chapter to create full-on, fantastic, guilt-free lunches and dinners. You could also snack on these throughout the day or serve them to people you like . . . totally your call!

four-cheese
stuffed-silly mushrooms

PER SERVING (6 stuffed mushrooms): 198 calories, 1.75g fat, 792mg sodium, 25g carbs, 4.5g fiber, 8.5g sugars, 22g protein

There's nothing silly about these mushrooms, except for how insanely overstuffed they are ... and the fact that they have so few calories (only 33 each). So stuff *yourself* silly with 'em.

Ingredients

6 medium-large baby bella mushrooms (each about 2 inches wide)
¼ cup fat-free ricotta cheese
¼ cup finely chopped onion
¼ cup canned spinach, thoroughly drained and dried
2 tablespoons fat-free cream cheese
2 tablespoons shredded fat-free mozzarella cheese
1 tablespoon minced garlic
1 teaspoon reduced-fat Parmesan-style grated topping
½ teaspoon garlic powder
⅛ teaspoon nutmeg
⅛ teaspoon salt

Directions

Preheat oven to 375 degrees.

Gently remove stems from mushrooms. Chop stems into small pieces and set aside.

With the rounded sides down, place mushroom caps on a baking sheet sprayed lightly with nonstick spray. Bake in the oven for 12 to 14 minutes. Do not turn oven off.

Meanwhile, bring a pan sprayed with nonstick spray to medium heat on the stove. Add chopped mushroom stems, onion, and garlic. Cook and stir until garlic is soft, about 3 minutes. Once mushroom caps are cool enough to handle, pat dry until free of all excess moisture. Set aside.

In a medium bowl, combine ricotta cheese, cream cheese, nutmeg, and salt until mixed well. Add mushroom-onion mixture, spinach, and mozzarella cheese. Stir until blended.

Evenly distribute cheese mixture among mushroom caps. They will be super-stuffed and the mixture will be piled on top, too!

In a small dish, mix Parm-style topping with garlic powder. Sprinkle stuffed mushrooms with this mixture.

Place stuffed mushrooms back in the oven and cook for 8 to 10 minutes, until topping begins to brown. Let cool slightly and enjoy!!!

MAKES 1 SERVING

HG Trivia Tidbit:

On average, Americans eat about half a pound of cheese a week. Whoa! We recommend you get your fix with these low-fat, cheesy mushrooms.

For Weight Watchers **POINTS**® values and photos of all the recipes in this book, check out hungry-girl.com/book.

cheesy butternut bake

PER SERVING (¼th of casserole): 101 calories, 1g fat, 457mg sodium, 20g carbs, 3g fiber, 5g sugars, 4g protein

Warning: This recipe is so good, you'll want to devour all four servings at once. So invite some friends over to share it with you . . . or break it up into individual servings before digging in.

Ingredients

4 cups cubed butternut squash
2 wedges The Laughing Cow Light Original Swiss cheese, room temperature
¾ cup diced onion
¼ cup fat-free liquid egg substitute
½ teaspoon salt
¼ teaspoon chili powder
⅛ teaspoon black pepper

Directions

Preheat oven to 350 degrees.

Place squash in a large microwave-safe bowl with ¼ cup water. Cover and microwave for 6 minutes. Once bowl is cool enough to handle, uncover and drain any excess water. Set aside.

Place onion in a small microwave-safe dish with 2 tablespoons water. Cover and microwave for 3 minutes. Let cool slightly, uncover and drain any excess water. Set aside.

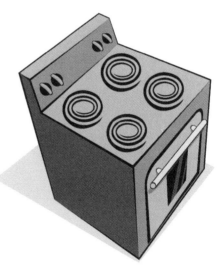

Place squash in a blender. Add all of the other ingredients except for the onion. Pulse until thoroughly mixed but not liquefied.

Remove blender from base and stir in onion. Transfer mixture to a small casserole dish sprayed with nonstick spray.

Bake in the oven for 35 to 40 minutes, until edges of the squash casserole begin to brown. Serve with a spoon as you would mashed potatoes.

MAKES 4 SERVINGS

Chew on This

The most popular variety of butternut squash, the Waltham butternut, originated in Stow, Massachusetts. The old farm is gone now, but in its place is the Butternut Farm Golf Club! Sounds like the people there may actually love squash as much as we do.

crunchy sassy chinese slaw

PER SERVING (about 1 cup): 111 calories, 3.5g fat, 375mg sodium, 17.5g carbs, 4g fiber, 10g sugars, 3g protein

This slaw is so sassy and so good that you may want to inhale multiple servings of it. But even eating HALF of this six-serving batch would only set you back 333 calories! Not too bad...

◌ Ingredients

HG Heads Up!
Don't miss our Scoopable Chinese Chicken Salad on page 77. It was inspired by several afternoons of adding chicken chunks to this slaw, turning it into a mini meal.

One 16-ounce package dry broccoli slaw mix
1 cup canned water chestnuts, drained and sliced into thin strips
1 cup canned mandarin orange segments packed in water or juice, drained and chopped (and rinsed, if packed in juice)
1 cup chopped scallions
⅔ cup Newman's Own Lighten Up! Low Fat Sesame Ginger Dressing
¼ cup slivered almonds

◌ Directions

In a large bowl, toss all ingredients together and mix well.

Refrigerate for at least 2 hours. Stir well before serving, then slaw it up!

MAKES 6 SERVINGS

bacon-bundled bbq shrimp

PER SERVING (4 pieces): 116 calories, 1.75g fat, 587mg sodium, 7g carbs, <0.5g fiber, 6g sugars, 16g protein

This is a fantastic party recipe! The shrimp, bacon, and BBQ sauce combo makes it nearly impossible for anyone to believe that these are guilt-free in any way. Yet each one has less than 30 calories!

 ## Ingredients

16 large (not jumbo) raw shrimp, peeled, deveined, tails removed
8 slices extra-lean turkey bacon, halved widthwise
⅓ cup canned tomato sauce
3 tablespoons ketchup
1 tablespoon brown sugar (not packed)
1 tablespoon cider vinegar
½ teaspoon garlic powder

Directions

Preheat oven to 425 degrees.

In a small bowl, combine tomato sauce, ketchup, sugar, vinegar, and garlic powder until mixed well. Set aside.

Lightly spray a baking sheet with nonstick spray. Take ½ slice bacon and coat it in the sauce. Wrap the sauce-covered bacon around a shrimp and place it, seam side down, on the baking sheet. Repeat with the rest of the bacon and shrimp. Give them a quick mist with nonstick spray.

Bake in the oven until shrimp are cooked through and bacon is crispy, 10 to 15 minutes.

MAKES 4 SERVINGS

 For a pic of this recipe, see the first photo insert. Yay!

spinach, mushroom, and mozzarella supreme

PER SERVING (⅛th of casserole): 106 calories, 1g fat, 597mg sodium, 11g carbs, 3.5g fiber, 4g sugars, 8g protein

Here's a side dish that's so good, you may want to make it into a meal by having a few servings. We've been known to plow through dishes of this stuff like there's no tomorrow.

Ingredients

Two 16-ounce bags frozen chopped spinach, thawed, drained, and thoroughly dried

1½ cups canned sliced mushrooms (about 2 medium cans or 1 large one), drained

3 wedges The Laughing Cow cheese (any Light flavor), room temperature

1 cup diced onion

⅓ cup shredded fat-free mozzarella cheese

¾ teaspoon garlic powder

Optional: salt and black pepper

Directions

Preheat oven to 350 degrees.

In a pan sprayed with nonstick spray, cook onion over high heat on the stove until browned, about 3 minutes. Set aside.

Pat spinach with paper towels, making sure all excess moisture has been removed. In a mixing bowl, combine spinach, onion, cheese wedges, and garlic powder. Mix well, until thoroughly combined.

Spray a medium casserole dish with nonstick spray. Spread half the spinach mixture along the bottom. Layer half the mushrooms evenly over the spinach mixture.

Spread remaining spinach mixture over the mushroom layer. Layer remaining mushrooms on top. Sprinkle casserole with mozzarella cheese.

Bake in the oven for 25 to 30 minutes, until cheese layer begins to crisp slightly.

Season to taste with salt and pepper, if you like.

MAKES 6 SERVINGS

HG Trivia Tidbit:

Crystal City, Texas, is strong to the finish and proud of it. In 1937, this spinach-growing community erected a statue of Popeye in honor of how popular he made their favorite leafy green veggie. However, the muscled-up sailor got no such love from the sweet potato community for his catchphrase, "I yam what I yam."

For Weight Watchers *POINTS*® values and photos of all the recipes in this book, check out hungry-girl.com/book.

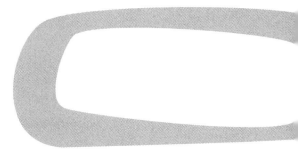

h-o-t hot boneless buffalo wings

If you like Buffalo wings, you'll love, love, love these spicy chicken nuggets. Dipping the chicken in Frank's RedHot makes these taste like REAL wings. It's hard to believe how low in fat and calories they are.

Ingredients

Heads up, F1 fans! Don't miss our Fun with Fiber One chapter, starting on page 282.

8 ounces raw boneless skinless lean chicken breast, cut into 10 nuggets

¼ cup Fiber One bran cereal (original)

1 ounce (about 14 crisps) Pringles Light Fat Free Barbeque Potato Crisps (or another fat-free BBQ-flavored potato chip)

3 tablespoons Frank's RedHot Original Cayenne Pepper Sauce

Dash onion powder

Dash garlic powder

Dash cayenne pepper

Dash black pepper

Dash salt

Directions

Preheat oven to 375 degrees.

In a blender or food processor, grind Fiber One to a breadcrumb-like consistency.

Crush potato crisps completely. In a small dish, mix crushed crisps with cereal crumbs. Add onion powder, garlic powder, cayenne, black pepper, and salt, and mix well.

Place chicken pieces in a separate dish. Cover with Frank's RedHot and toss to coat.

Spray a baking sheet with nonstick spray. Give each chicken piece a shake so it's not dripping with sauce, and then coat evenly with crumb mixture. Lay crumb-covered nuggets on the baking sheet.

Bake in the oven for 10 minutes.

Flip nuggets over and bake for 10 more minutes, or until outsides are crispy and chicken is cooked throughout.

MAKES 2 SERVINGS

📷 For a pic of this recipe, see the first photo insert. Yay!

Chew on This

Sources say that in 1964, Teressa Bellissimo was faced with whipping up a late-night snack for her son and his friends. The result of this culinary improvisation was the hot wing recipe we all know and love. She soon put them on the menu at her bar in Buffalo, New York, and sealed her place in Hungry Girl history!

lean-o cioppino

PER SERVING (1 generous cup): 190 calories, 3.25g fat,
1,006mg sodium, 23g carbs, 1.5g fiber, 13.5g sugars, 17g protein

Cioppino is a fish stew and it's soooo good. This recipe is ridiculously easy to make, yet it tastes like a lot of work went into it. The best canned soup for this is definitely Amy's Organic Chunky Tomato Bisque!

Ingredients

2 cups creamy tomato soup with 4g fat or less per serving
⅓ cup canned or pouched whole baby clams, drained
3 ounces cooked medium-small shrimp (about 10 shrimp)

Directions

Combine all ingredients in a pot or microwave-safe bowl.

On the stove or in the microwave, bring stew to desired heat. Enjoy!

MAKES 2 SERVINGS

> **HG Tip!** If salt's a concern, look for a low-sodium canned soup—you can easily save hundreds of milligrams of sodium that way.

cheesy-good cornbread muffins

PER SERVING (1 muffin): 85 calories, 1.5g fat, 240mg sodium, 14g carbs, 1g fiber, 2g sugars, 4g protein

These don't taste particularly cheesy—they're actually sweet and completely fantastic. Hard to believe they only have 85 calories each...

 Ingredients

1 cup canned cream-style corn
⅔ cup all-purpose flour
½ cup yellow cornmeal
½ cup fat-free liquid egg substitute
½ cup fat-free sour cream
½ cup shredded reduced-fat cheddar cheese
¼ cup chopped scallions
2 tablespoons Splenda No Calorie Sweetener (granulated)
1½ teaspoons baking powder
¼ teaspoon salt
Optional: ¼ teaspoon hot sauce

Directions

Preheat oven to 375 degrees.

In a large bowl, combine flour, cornmeal, Splenda, baking powder, and salt until mixed well.

In a small bowl, mix together all of the other ingredients: corn, egg substitute, sour cream, cheese, and scallions. Add the hot sauce, if you like.

Add contents of the small bowl to the large one and stir until mixed thoroughly.

Line a 12-cup muffin pan with baking cups and/or spray with nonstick spray. Evenly distribute muffin batter among the cups.

Bake in the oven for 15 to 20 minutes, until muffins are firm and light golden brown. Allow to cool for a few minutes, and then enjoy!

MAKES 12 SERVINGS

butternut hash browns

PER SERVING (about 1 cup): 104 calories, 3g fat, 162mg sodium, 20g carbs, 3g fiber, 5g sugars, 2g protein

These are an insanely fantastic addition to any egg dish. Zazzle up your plate—they're great as a side with breakfast, lunch, or dinner!

Ingredients

1 heaping cup shredded butternut squash
2 tablespoons chopped onion
¼ teaspoon onion powder
¼ teaspoon garlic powder
Dash salt
Dash black pepper
Olive oil nonstick spray
Additional salt and black pepper, to taste
Optional toppings: ketchup, salsa, hot sauce

Directions

Spread shredded squash out between 2 layers of paper towels. Press down to absorb as much moisture from squash as possible. Repeat if necessary, until no more water can be removed.

In a medium bowl, toss squash shreds with onion, onion powder, garlic powder, salt, and pepper until mixed well.

Mist a small to medium pan with a 2-second spray of olive oil nonstick spray. Bring to high heat.

Add squash mixture to the pan. Remove from heat and top with another 2-second spray of the olive oil spray. Return to heat and cook for 2 minutes.

Flip shreds with a spatula. Cook for another 2 minutes or so, until mixture is thoroughly cooked and browned.

Plate your HBs, and season to taste with more salt and pepper.

Finish off with one of our optional toppings, if you like.

MAKES 1 SERVING

HG Tip! Use a cheese grater to get perfectly shredded b-nut squash.

Chew on This

A side order of hash browns from Denny's packs in 12 grams fat and around 200 calories. And it's typically served alongside an entrée of cheesy eggs, buttered toast, and some kind of salty, fatty meat. Um, no thanks!

sassy southwestern egg rolls

PER SERVING (3 egg roll halves with sauce): 181 calories, 4.5g fat, 666mg sodium, 27g carbs, 14g fiber, 2g sugars, 19g protein

Here's our take on the zesty egg rolls made famous by Chili's. These are really delicious—and they have a teeny tiny fraction of the fat compared to the Chili's version. Yeah, we're good!

Ingredients

For Egg Rolls
3 original (not large) La Tortilla Factory Smart & Delicious Low Carb/High Fiber tortillas
1 ounce cooked skinless lean chicken breast, shredded
¾ cup frozen chopped spinach, thawed and thoroughly drained
2 tablespoons canned black beans
2 tablespoons canned sweet corn, drained
1 ounce fat-free jalapeño jack cheese, shredded
1 tablespoon diced red chili pepper

For Sauce
2 tablespoons fat-free sour cream
1 tablespoon mashed avocado
1 tablespoon diced tomato
½ teaspoon dry ranch dressing/dip mix
Black pepper, to taste

Directions

Preheat oven to 400 degrees.

In a small microwave-safe bowl, combine chicken, spinach, beans, corn, cheese, and chili pepper. Heat for 30 seconds in the microwave.

Warm tortillas in the microwave for 15 seconds. On a clean, flat surface, lay out tortillas side by side. Place one-third of the chicken-spinach mixture in the center of each tortilla.

To assemble each egg roll, fold sides in, so none of the filling can escape during cooking, and roll up from the bottom of the tortilla.

Place all three rolls seam side down on a baking sheet sprayed with nonstick cooking spray.

Bake in the oven for 12 minutes, flipping rolls over about halfway through cooking. Egg rolls should be crispy when done.

Meanwhile, in a small bowl, combine sour cream, avocado, and ranch mix. Stir until smooth and blended. Season to taste with black pepper.

Once egg rolls are done baking, allow them to cool for a few minutes. Cut each in half on a diagonal and arrange them beautifully on a plate.

Top dipping sauce with the diced tomato and serve with your egg rolls. Mmmmm!

MAKES 2 SERVINGS

For a pic of this recipe, see the first photo insert. Yay!

HG Fast Fact:

We've always known Chili's little Southwestern Egg Roll appetizer is fatty. But 810 calories and 51 grams of fat for three little rolls!?! That's NUTS! These have sane stats and are just as delicious. Promise!

miracle mashies

This recipe will keep any and every mashed potato fan happy. And that is a promise!

Ingredients

1 large potato (about 13 ounces)
3 cups cauliflower florets
3 tablespoons fat-free half & half
1 tablespoon light whipped butter or light buttery spread
¼ teaspoon salt
Additional salt, black pepper, to taste
Optional: ½ teaspoon crushed garlic

Directions

Bring a large pot of water to a boil. While waiting for water to boil, peel and cube potato.

Once water is boiling, add peeled potato cubes and cauliflower florets. Allow water to return to a boil, and then reduce heat to medium. Cook for 15 to 20 minutes, until potatoes and cauliflower are very tender.

Remove pot from heat and carefully drain water. Transfer potato mixture to a large bowl. Add half & half, butter, and salt. Add the crushed garlic, if you like.

Mash with a potato masher, until completely blended. Season to taste with pepper and additional salt. Enjoy!

MAKES 5 SERVINGS

cheesy "broc star" soup

PER SERVING (1 cup): 125 calories, 5.75g fat, 796mg sodium, 11.5g carbs, 2g fiber, 4.5g sugars, 7g protein

Almost too easy to make, this soup is creamy and decadent. It tastes super-fattening, but of course, it's not (it wouldn't be in this book if it was!). Pair it with a salad for a fantastic lunch.

Ingredients

1 tray Green Giant Just for One! Broccoli & Cheese Sauce
½ cup plain light soymilk
1 wedge The Laughing Cow Light Original Swiss cheese, chopped into pieces
Salt and black pepper, to taste

Directions

To prepare Broccoli & Cheese Sauce, pull film back slightly to vent. Microwave for 1½ minutes.

Pull film back all the way but do not remove, and stir in cheese wedge pieces.

Place film back over the tray and microwave for an additional 45 seconds. Mix well, and then allow to cool slightly.

Place broccoli-cheese mixture in a blender with soymilk. Blend at medium speed until desired consistency is reached. (Blend very briefly if you like broccoli pieces in your soup—blend longer for fully pureed soup.)

Transfer soup to your favorite microwave-safe bowl (or your second-favorite one, if your fave isn't clean). Heat soup in the microwave for 45 seconds, or until hot.

Season to taste with salt and pepper. Then slurp it up!

MAKES 1 SERVING

bacon 'n cheese bell pepper skins

PER SERVING (2 pieces): 119 calories, 5.5g fat, 378mg sodium, 6.5g carbs, 1.25g fiber, 3.5g sugars, 11g protein

These are JUST like potato skins but without all the starchy carbs, grease, oil, and other unnecessary items. You won't believe how satisfying and fantastic they are!

Ingredients

2 bell peppers (red, yellow, or orange)
6 slices extra-lean turkey bacon
¾ cup shredded reduced-fat cheddar cheese
¼ cup chopped scallions
¼ cup fat-free sour cream

Directions

Preheat oven to 350 degrees.

Cut peppers in half. Remove stems and seeds. Slice each pepper into quarters and set aside.

Spray a large baking sheet with nonstick spray. Place pepper slices on the sheet cut side up. Bake in the oven for about 20 minutes, until slices are soft.

Meanwhile, bring a large pan sprayed with nonstick spray to medium heat on the stove. Cook bacon on both sides until crispy. Let cool, and then chop into small pieces.

Once pepper slices are done, remove from the oven and let cool slightly. Don't turn off the oven. Blot away any excess liquid from peppers.

Sprinkle pepper slices evenly with shredded cheese, scallions, and chopped bacon. Return to the oven and bake until cheese has melted, 5 to 10 minutes. Serve with sour cream.

MAKES 4 SERVINGS

Chew on This

Let's say you order an appetizer of potato skins and split it with friends. Even three li'l skins will set you back around 300 calories and 17 grams of fat. And that's BEFORE you even get your main dish. There's nothing "skinny" about that!

mmmm-azing mini mushroom tartlets

Each of these delicious things has just 24 calories! BTW, these are best eaten the day they're prepared, which shouldn't be a problem since they're irresistible.

Ingredients

15 mini phyllo dough shells (found in the freezer aisle)
1 cup finely chopped portabello mushrooms
⅓ cup finely chopped white onion
3 tablespoons chopped scallions
3 tablespoons fat-free cream cheese, room temperature
½ teaspoon minced garlic
⅛ teaspoon salt
2 dashes black pepper
2 dashes nutmeg

Directions

Preheat oven to 375 degrees.

Bring a pan sprayed with nonstick spray to medium-high heat on the stove. Add mushrooms and onion, and cook until soft.

Place mushrooms and onion in a small bowl. Add scallions, cream cheese, garlic, salt, pepper, and nutmeg, and mix well.

Evenly distribute mushroom mixture among the phyllo shells. Arrange shells on a baking sheet sprayed lightly with nonstick spray. Bake in the oven for 12 to 15 minutes, until edges of tartlets are crisp.

Allow to cool slightly before serving. Yum!

MAKES 3 SERVINGS

 For a pic of this recipe, see the first photo insert. Yay!

For Weight Watchers *POINTS*®
values and photos of all the
recipes in this book, check out
hungry-girl.com/book.

cheesy cauliflower casserole

PER SERVING (1 generous cup): 117 calories, 2g fat, 668mg sodium, 10g carbs, 2.5g fiber, 6g sugars, 14.5g protein

It took a bazillion tries to get this one perfect, people. It was totally worth all the work, though. Even humans who don't like cauliflower will probably fall in love with this dish.

Ingredients

1 large head cauliflower, chopped (or 7 cups pre-chopped raw cauliflower)
1 onion, chopped
3 wedges The Laughing Cow Light Original Swiss cheese, room temperature
1 cup fat-free cottage cheese
1 cup low-fat or light ricotta cheese
1 cup shredded fat-free cheddar cheese
1 cup fat-free liquid egg substitute
1 teaspoon salt
⅛ teaspoon black pepper
Optional topping: paprika

Directions

Preheat oven to 375 degrees.

Place cauliflower and onion in a large microwave-safe bowl with ½ cup water. Cover and microwave for 6 to 8 minutes. Once bowl is cool enough to handle, drain water and set aside.

Place cheese wedges in a microwave-safe dish and microwave for 10 to 15 seconds. Mix until smooth. If needed, return to the microwave for an additional 10 seconds, and then stir again.

Add cheese and all of the other ingredients to the bowl with the cauliflower and onion, and stir until mixed well.

Spray a medium-large baking dish with nonstick spray. Transfer contents of the bowl to the baking dish. Sprinkle paprika lightly on top, if you like. Bake in the oven for 1 hour.

Let cool for at least 10 minutes. Serve warm or at room temperature.

MAKES 9 SERVINGS

HG Trivia Tidbit:

Most of us are used to plain old white cauliflower, but it also grows in green, orange, yellow, brown, and even purple varieties. Put 'em all together, and you've got one amazing Technicolor casserole. Or, um, just a scary gray one.

devilish eggs

PER SERVING (4 pieces): 79 calories, 1.75g fat, 403mg sodium, 6.25g carbs, 1g fiber, 2.5g sugars, 9.5g protein

Deviled eggs are no longer a fatty no-no. This recipe will have you churning out creamy, delicious eggs in no time.

Ingredients

2 cups roughly chopped orange cauliflower

10 hard-boiled eggs, chilled

3 wedges The Laughing Cow Light Original Swiss cheese, room temperature

¼ cup fat-free mayonnaise

1 tablespoon sweet relish, patted dry to remove moisture

2 teaspoons minced shallots

1½ teaspoons yellow mustard

Salt and black pepper, to taste

Optional topping: paprika

Directions

Place cauliflower in a large microwave-safe bowl with ⅓ cup water. Cover and microwave for 6 to 8 minutes, until cauliflower is soft.

Once bowl is cool enough to handle, drain any excess water from cauliflower.

Lightly mash cauliflower, and then place in a blender. Add mayo and puree until just blended, not smooth. Do not over-blend.

In a mixing bowl, combine cauliflower mixture with cheese wedges, relish, mustard, and shallots. Stir until smooth. Season mixture to taste with salt and pepper. Refrigerate for at least 1 hour.

When ready to serve, halve eggs lengthwise and remove yolks. Evenly distribute cauliflower mixture among egg white halves and, if you like, top with paprika.

MAKES 5 SERVINGS

📷 For a pic of this recipe, see the first photo insert. Yay!

HG Tip! This recipe calls for orange cauliflower. If you can't find it, use regular cauliflower. But add a drop of yellow food coloring to the mixture if you want your Devilish Eggs to look like the real thing.

For Weight Watchers **POINTS**®
values and photos of all the
recipes in this book, check out
hungry-girl.com/book.

chapter five

dip it good

Sauces, Dips, and Dippers

The recipes in this chapter are very unique. The idea here was to create a bunch of great sauces and dips that could be enjoyed with veggies, meats, and store-bought items. But we also wanted to give you some simple yet amazing recipes for things you can *dip* into these special sauces and dips (or even eat straight!). It's all about variety and mixing things up. Dig in!

HUNGRY

BOWL XX

not-so-secret bbq sauce

PER SERVING (about 3 tablespoons): 37 calories, 0g fat,
347mg sodium, 9g carbs, 0.5g fiber, 8g sugars, <1g protein

It's not a secret anymore. Here's a sauce you'll end up putting on EVERYTHING.

Ingredients

¼ cup canned tomato sauce

2 tablespoons ketchup

2 teaspoons brown sugar (not packed)

2 teaspoons cider vinegar

½ teaspoon garlic powder

Directions

Combine ingredients and mix well. That's it!

MAKES 2 SERVINGS

For Weight Watchers *POINTS*®
values and photos of all the
recipes in this book, check out
hungry-girl.com/book.

just fondue it

PER SERVING (about 3 tablespoons): 89 calories, 2.5g fat, 548mg sodium, 3g carbs, 0g fiber, 2g sugars, 10g protein

The secret here is mixing a couple of fat-free items with ones that are just low in fat. The result is creamy, cheesy, gooey fondue that's so good, you'll want to swim in it!

Ingredients

¼ cup plus 1 tablespoon plain light soymilk
3 ounces fat-free cheddar cheese (in block form)
2 wedges The Laughing Cow Light Original Swiss cheese
2 slices reduced-fat Swiss cheese, torn into pieces
2 tablespoons fat-free cream cheese
2 tablespoons dry white wine
½ teaspoon minced garlic
Dash salt

Directions

Bring a saucepan sprayed with nonstick spray to medium-low heat. Add garlic and cook for 1 minute.

Add soymilk, all four cheeses, and salt. Cook for 3 to 4 minutes, stirring continuously, until cheeses have melted and sauce is mixed thoroughly.

Reduce heat to low and add wine. Stir until combined. Transfer mixture to a fondue pot and set temperature to low. Dive in!

MAKES 4 SERVINGS

hungry, hungry artichoke hummus

PER SERVING (¼ cup): 56 calories, 0.5g fat, 400mg sodium, 9g carbs, 3g fiber, 1g sugars, 3g protein

Ohhhhh ... artichokes and hummus are quite the little couple. Don't believe it? MAKE THIS DIP!

Ingredients

One 15-ounce can chickpeas (garbanzo beans), drained
1 cup canned artichoke hearts, drained
¼ cup fat-free vegetable broth
¼ cup plain fat-free Greek yogurt
1 tablespoon lemon juice
1½ teaspoons crushed garlic
½ teaspoon dried parsley flakes
½ teaspoon salt
¼ teaspoon black pepper
¼ teaspoon ground cumin
¼ teaspoon paprika
Optional garnish: additional parsley flakes and paprika

Directions

Place all ingredients except for chickpeas in a blender.

Using a potato masher or a fork, thoroughly mash chickpeas. Transfer to the blender. Puree until smooth, stopping and stirring if blending slows.

For best flavor, refrigerate hummus for several hours. Before serving, garnish with a sprinkle each of paprika and parsley flakes, if you like.

MAKES 8 SERVINGS

hint of mint
yogurty cucumber dip

PER SERVING (¼ cup): 17 calories, 0g fat, 198mg sodium,
3g carbs, 0.5g fiber, 1g sugars, 1g protein

Our pals at Weight Watchers know a lot about tasty dips and dressings. This concoction is great to dunk carrots into and also as a salad dressing. It's creamy, oniony and, like the name promises, has a hint of mint!

This recipe was co-developed with Weight Watchers®.

Ingredients

4 ounces plain fat-free Greek yogurt
1 medium English cucumber, chopped
1 cup chopped red onion
1 cup fresh mint leaves
1 teaspoon salt
⅛ teaspoon sugar
1 to 3 cloves garlic, to taste

Directions

Combine all ingredients in a food processor or blender. Blend until your desired consistency is reached.

Refrigerate for at least 2 hours (overnight is best). Enjoy!

MAKES 12 SERVINGS

holy moly guacamole

PER SERVING (⅓ cup): 78 calories, 3g fat, 320mg sodium,
10.5g carbs, 3.5g fiber, 4g sugars, 3.5g protein

*Don't let the peas scare you. This stuff tastes like regular guacamole.
Use it as a dip, on omelettes, or as a spread for sandwiches.*

Ingredients

One 15-ounce can early (young) peas, drained
½ cup mashed avocado (about 1 medium-small avocado's worth)
⅓ cup chopped cherry or grape tomatoes
¼ cup finely chopped onion
¼ cup plain fat-free Greek yogurt
4 teaspoons lime juice
½ teaspoon chopped garlic
½ teaspoon garlic powder
¼ teaspoon salt
⅛ teaspoon black pepper
⅛ teaspoon ground cumin
⅛ teaspoon chili powder
Additional salt and black pepper, to taste
Optional: chopped fresh cilantro, chopped jarred jalapeños

Directions

Place peas in a medium bowl and
mash thoroughly with a potato
masher or fork.

Add avocado, yogurt, lime juice,
garlic, and seasonings. Continue
to mash until blended.

Stir in tomatoes, onion, and, if you like, some cilantro and/or jalapeños. Season to taste with salt and pepper. Enjoy!

MAKES 6 SERVINGS

📷 For a pic of this recipe, see the first photo insert. Yay!

HG Fast Fact:

Avocados aren't just delicious. Spanish conquistadors used the liquid from the avocado seeds to make reddish-blackish ink. Hmmm, wonder if we should think about printing the next HG book with avocado ink . . .

crazy-creamy spinach artichoke dip

This dip really IS crazy-creamy. No exaggeration here.

Ingredients

One 10-ounce package frozen chopped spinach, thawed and drained thoroughly
One 14-ounce can artichoke hearts packed in water, drained thoroughly and chopped
One 8-ounce container fat-free cream cheese, room temperature
One-half 8-ounce can water chestnuts, drained and chopped
¼ cup fat-free sour cream
¼ cup fat-free mayonnaise
¼ cup reduced-fat Parmesan-style grated topping, divided
3 tablespoons minced shallots
2 cloves garlic, minced
¼ teaspoon salt
⅛ teaspoon cayenne pepper

Directions

If you want to serve this dish hot, preheat oven to 350 degrees.

In a large bowl, combine cream cheese, sour cream, mayo, and 3 tablespoons Parm-style topping until mixed well. Add salt and cayenne pepper, and stir until smooth.

In a pan sprayed with nonstick spray, cook shallots and garlic over medium heat on the stove until soft, 1 to 2 minutes. Set aside.

To the large bowl, add spinach, artichoke hearts, water chestnuts, and garlic-shallot mixture, and stir well.

If serving dip cold, top with remaining 1 tablespoon Parm-style topping and you're done!

If serving dip hot, transfer to a medium casserole dish, top with remaining Parm-style topping, and then bake in the oven for about 30 minutes, until bubbly. Let cool slightly before serving.

MAKES 8 SERVINGS

Chew on This

Catherine de Médicis is credited as the gal who introduced artichokes to France. According to a royal chronicler, she ate so much at a courtier's wedding that she "thought she would die, and was very ill." We've been there, Catherine.

fluffy cinnamon–cream cheese dip

PER SERVING (3 tablespoons): 43 calories, <0.5g fat, 107mg sodium, 6.5g carbs, 0g fiber, 2g sugars, 2.5g protein

This is like a cross between sweet cinnamon frosting and a slice of cheesecake. And it's soooo easy to make!

Ingredients

¾ cup Cool Whip Free, thawed
¼ cup fat-free cream cheese, room temperature
3 tablespoons Splenda No Calorie Sweetener (granulated)
¼ teaspoon cinnamon

Directions

Combine all ingredients in a bowl. Mix until thoroughly blended and smooth.

Chill for at least 10 minutes before dipping!

MAKES 4 SERVINGS

HG Trivia Tidbit:

Cinnamon is actually one of the flavors in cola. See, it really IS in everything!

For Weight Watchers *POINTS*® values and photos of all the recipes in this book, check out hungry-girl.com/book.

sweet cinnamon pita chips

PER SERVING (12 chips): 144 calories, 2.5g fat, 290mg sodium, 27.5g carbs, 6g fiber, 1g sugars, 5g protein

Looking for the crunch of a cracker with the sweetness of a dessert? These are GREAT for dipping. Try 'em with our Fluffy Cinnamon–Cream Cheese Dip (page 116) and our Chunky Caramel-Apple Pumpkin Dip (page 118)!

Ingredients

1 whole-wheat or high-fiber pita
1 teaspoon Splenda No Calorie Sweetener (granulated)
½ teaspoon cinnamon
Butter-flavored nonstick spray

Directions

Preheat oven to 350 degrees.

In a small dish, combine Splenda and cinnamon. Mix well and set aside.

Slice pita into six wedges. Carefully open up each wedge and separate into two triangles.

Lightly spray a baking sheet with nonstick spray. Arrange triangles flat on the sheet with the inner part of the pita facing up.

Cover pita triangles with a 1-second spray of butter-flavored spray. Immediately sprinkle with Splenda-cinnamon mixture. Give pita triangles another 1-second mist of butter-flavored spray.

Bake in the oven for 5 to 7 minutes, or until triangles are crispy.

MAKES 1 SERVING

chunky caramel-apple pumpkin dip

PER SERVING (¼ cup): 52 calories, <0.5g fat, 96mg sodium,
11.5g carbs, 1.25g fiber, 4.5g sugars, <0.5g protein

Oh, boy! This stuff is so good, we teared up the first time it was sampled at the HG HQ. Use it as a dip, or just spoon it into your mouth straight and enjoy it as a dessert. A full cup has just over 200 calories! Get ready to cry pumpkin-inspired tears of joy. Pssst ... it's even better the day after it's prepared!

Ingredients

HG Heads Up!
Love apples? Do not miss the Fun with Fujis chapter, starting on page 266.

One 8-ounce container Cool Whip Free, thawed

One 15-ounce can pure pumpkin

1 small (4-serving) package sugar-free fat-free vanilla instant pudding mix

2 cups finely diced apples

1 tablespoon Splenda No Calorie Sweetener (granulated)

2 teaspoons fat-free caramel dip

2 teaspoons cornstarch

1 teaspoon pumpkin pie spice

1 teaspoon vanilla extract, divided

½ teaspoon cinnamon

Dash salt

Directions

Place apples in a microwave-safe dish with ¼ cup water. Cover and microwave for 2½ minutes. Once dish is cool enough to handle, drain water and set aside.

Place ½ cup cold water in a small saucepan. Add Splenda, cornstarch, cinnamon, ½ teaspoon of the vanilla extract, and salt, and mix thoroughly.

Bring the saucepan to medium-low heat, then stir in caramel dip. Continue cooking, stirring occasionally, until mixture is hot, thick, and bubbly, about 5 minutes. Then add the apples and stir until mixed. Refrigerate until cold, about 1 hour.

Meanwhile, mix pumpkin pie spice and remaining ½ teaspoon vanilla extract into the Cool Whip.

In a large bowl, combine vanilla pudding mix with pure pumpkin and stir well. Fold in Cool Whip mixture, making sure it is completely blended. Refrigerate.

Once caramel-y apples are cold, stir them into the chilled pumpkin mixture. Store dip in the refrigerator until ready to serve. Mmmmmm!

MAKES 16 SERVINGS

mostly roasted veggie explosion

PER SERVING (⅛th of platter): 71 calories, <0.5g fat, 97mg sodium, 15.5g carbs, 7g fiber, 6g sugars, 3g protein

This platter is abnormally large and SUPER-DELICIOUS. Chew your veggies straight, or dip 'em in any number of our dips. (Pssst ... we recommend the Sweet Caramelized Onion Dip on page 122!)

Ingredients

1 pound asparagus
1 eggplant, ends removed
1 red bell pepper
1 yellow bell pepper
3 large carrots, peeled and cut into ½-inch-wide sticks
1 small jicama, peeled and cut into ½-inch-wide sticks
2 cups sugar snap peas
6 to 8 cherry tomatoes
6 to 8 fresh basil leaves
¼ teaspoon salt

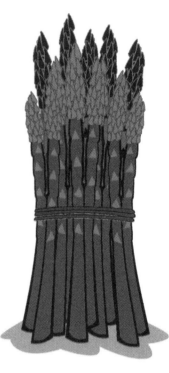

Directions

Preheat oven to 400 degrees.

Cut eggplant lengthwise into six to eight ¼-inch slices. Blot excess moisture from slices with paper towels. Sprinkle both sides with the salt.

Spray a baking sheet with nonstick spray. Arrange eggplant slices flat on the sheet. Bake for about 15 minutes, flipping slices halfway through cooking, until slices are soft but not crispy. Remove from sheet and set aside to cool.

Raise oven temperature to 425 degrees.

Re-spray the baking sheet. Break each asparagus stalk where it naturally snaps and discard the tough ends. Lay asparagus on the sheet. Bake for about 7 minutes for thin stalks or about 15 minutes for thick stalks, flipping them halfway through cooking. Remove from sheet and set aside to cool.

Re-spray sheet and lay carrot sticks flat on the sheet. Bake for about 14 minutes, flipping sticks halfway through cooking, until carrots are slightly browned but still firm.

Meanwhile, remove stems and seeds from both peppers. Cut into ½-inch-thick slices.

Re-spray sheet and arrange pepper slices flat on the sheet. Bake for about 10 minutes, flipping slices halfway through cooking. Remove from sheet and set aside to cool.

To assemble, place one basil leaf lengthwise on an eggplant slice. Add a cherry tomato at the short base of the slice. Roll eggplant up from the bottom, around the tomato, and secure with a toothpick. Repeat with all of the other eggplant slices.

Refrigerate asparagus, carrots, pepper slices, and eggplant rolls until completely chilled, at least 1 hour.

When it's time to serve, arrange the chilled roasted veggies on a platter with the jicama and sugar snap peas.

MAKES 8 SERVINGS

HG Tip! Think raw sugar snap peas taste too "grassy"? Feel free to soften them a bit in the microwave—just place them in a dish with 2 tablespoons water, cover, and nuke for 1 to 2 minutes.

sweet caramelized onion dip

PER SERVING (⅓ cup): 74 calories, 1.75g fat, 512mg sodium, 11g carbs, 0.5g fiber, 4.5g sugars, 3.5g protein

This onion dip is better than ANY onion dip EVER. Seriously. There is no better onion dip anywhere. Try it and see for yourself. BTW, you can eat it with chips, crackers, veggies . . . even on sandwiches and wraps. YUM!!!

Ingredients

HG Heads Up!
This tastes better after several hours in the fridge, so for best results make it the day before you plan to eat it.

2 large sweet onions, chopped

6 tablespoons fat-free cream cheese, room temperature

½ cup fat-free sour cream

½ cup fat-free mayonnaise

1 tablespoon light whipped butter or light buttery spread

1 teaspoon Dijon mustard

1 teaspoon balsamic vinegar

¼ teaspoon cayenne pepper

½ teaspoon salt

Directions

Heat butter in a large pan over medium-high heat. Once butter has coated the bottom of the pan, add onions, cayenne pepper, and salt. Don't worry if onions are piled high in the pan—they will cook down. Sauté for 10 minutes, stirring often.

Reduce heat to medium-low, and cook for an additional 25 to 30 minutes, stirring occasionally, until onions are browned and caramelized.

Meanwhile, in a large bowl, combine cream cheese, sour cream, and mayo. Whisk until smooth, then refrigerate.

Once onions are caramelized, add mustard and vinegar to the pan. Continue to cook for 5 minutes, stirring frequently. Remove onions from heat and allow to cool.

Once cool, add onions to the large bowl and mix dip thoroughly. Refrigerate overnight to allow flavors to combine. Serve at room temperature.

MAKES 6 SERVINGS

For a pic of this recipe, see the first photo insert. Yay!

For Weight Watchers *POINTS*®
values and photos of all the
recipes in this book, check out
hungry-girl.com/book.

kickin' peanut sauce

Regular Thai peanut sauce is a fatty mess. This version is sweet and nutty yet has WAY fewer calories and a tiny fraction of the fat the regular stuff has.

Ingredients

⅓ cup plus 2 tablespoons plain light soymilk
¼ cup plain fat-free yogurt
1½ tablespoons reduced-fat peanut butter, room temperature
1½ tablespoons light/low-sodium soy sauce
1½ tablespoons soy nuts, crushed
1 no-calorie sweetener packet
¼ teaspoon crushed garlic
¼ teaspoon dried minced onion
⅛ teaspoon cayenne pepper

Directions

Place all ingredients except for yogurt in a small saucepan. Bring to medium-low heat. Stirring constantly, cook until ingredients are thoroughly blended.

Remove from heat and let cool.

Mix in the yogurt, stirring until sauce is lump-free. Enjoy hot, warm, or cold!

MAKES 5 SERVINGS

HG Trivia Tidbit:

The comic strip *Peanuts* ran from October 2, 1950, to February 13, 2000. During those 50 years, 17,897 strips were published. The strips still run in syndication, and we still watch *A Charlie Brown Christmas* every year.

zesty italian pita chips

PER SERVING (12 chips): 163 calories, 4.5g fat, 453mg sodium, 27g carbs, 5.5g fiber, 1.5g sugars, 5g protein

If you're tired of boring pita chips, spice 'em up Italian-style. It's easy!

Ingredients

1 whole-wheat or high-fiber pita

2 teaspoons light whipped butter or light buttery spread, room temperature

2 teaspoons fat-free Italian dressing

½ teaspoon dried parsley flakes

¼ teaspoon lemon juice

¼ teaspoon crushed garlic

¼ teaspoon minced dried onion

Directions

Preheat oven to 400 degrees.

Slice pita into six wedges. Carefully open up each wedge and separate into two triangles.

Spray a baking sheet lightly with nonstick spray. Arrange triangles flat on the sheet, with the inner part of the pita facing up.

In a small dish, combine all of the other ingredients, stirring until mostly mixed. Don't worry if butter and Italian dressing do not fully integrate.

Evenly spread buttery mixture over pita triangles. Bake in the oven for 5 to 7 minutes, or until triangles are crispy. Serve hot, warm, or room temperature.

MAKES 1 SERVING

mexican bean & cheese dip

PER SERVING (about ⅓ cup): 87 calories, 0.5g fat,
441mg sodium, 10g carbs, 3g fiber, 1g sugars, 10.5g protein

This dip is a big, beany, cheesy pile of fun!

Ingredients

1 cup frozen ground-beef-style soy crumbles
½ cup fat-free refried beans
½ cup canned black beans, drained
½ cup shredded fat-free cheddar cheese
¼ cup fat-free cream cheese, room temperature
¼ cup chopped scallions
¼ cup canned tomatoes with green chilies, drained
¼ cup chopped fresh tomatoes
1 tablespoon taco sauce
¼ teaspoon dry taco seasoning mix
Optional topping: fat-free sour cream

Directions

In a medium microwave-safe dish, combine soy crumbles with taco seasoning and taco sauce until well mixed. Heat in the microwave for 30 seconds, then set aside.

In a small dish, combine cream cheese with refried beans and mix well.

Spray an 8-inch by 8-inch microwave-safe baking dish (glass is best) with nonstick spray.

Layer the cheesy bean mixture on the bottom. Spread soy crumble mixture on top.

In another dish, combine black beans, scallions, canned tomatoes with chilies, and fresh tomatoes. Evenly spread this mixture in a layer on top of the "meat" mixture.

Sprinkle cheddar cheese over the entire dish. Loosely cover with microwave-safe plastic wrap. Microwave for 5 minutes, or until cheese has melted. Top with sour cream, if desired, and serve with your favorite dippers!

MAKES 6 SERVINGS

HG Tip! This is one of those great, prepare-ahead-of-time dishes. Prep the dish, cover with plastic wrap, and leave it in your fridge until the party starts. Then just pop it in the microwave and serve!

creamy vanilla dip

PER SERVING (2 tablespoons): 34 calories, 0g fat, 96mg sodium,
5.5g carbs, 0g fiber, 1.5g sugars, 1.5g protein

Dipping fruit in this stuff makes an ordinary low-calorie snack feel
like a super-indulgent dessert. Make this dip often, people!

Ingredients

¾ cup Cool Whip Free, thawed
3 tablespoons fat-free cream cheese, room temperature
3 tablespoons Splenda No Calorie Sweetener (granulated)
½ tablespoon sugar-free fat-free vanilla instant pudding mix

Directions

In a mixing bowl, combine all ingredients. Stir until smooth and blended.

Refrigerate for at least 30 minutes before serving. Enjoy!

MAKES 5 SERVINGS

nacho-average tortilla chips

PER SERVING (12 chips): 126 calories, 3g fat, 217mg sodium, 22.5g carbs, 3g fiber, <0.5g sugars, 2.5g protein

These are cheesy, fiber-packed, and delicious, and they have WAY less fat than your average nacho chips. Homemade Doritos, anyone?!

Ingredients

2 small corn tortillas
1 teaspoon fat-free cheese-flavored sprinkles
¼ teaspoon dry taco seasoning mix
Two 1-second sprays nonstick spray

Directions

Preheat oven to 400 degrees.

In a small dish, combine cheese sprinkles with taco seasoning and mix well.

Cut each tortilla in half. Cut each half into three triangles.

Spray a baking sheet lightly with nonstick spray. Arrange tortilla triangles close together on the sheet.

Cover triangles with a 1-second spray of nonstick spray. Evenly sprinkle half the seasoning mixture over triangles.

Flip triangles over. Again, cover with a 1-second spray of nonstick spray. Sprinkle remaining seasoning mixture over triangles.

Bake in the oven for 4 minutes. Carefully flip tortilla triangles over on the sheet.

Bake in the oven for an additional 4 minutes, until chips are crispy.

MAKES 1 SERVING

 For a pic of this recipe, see the first photo insert. Yay!

peachy-cream fruity fondue

PER SERVING (¼ cup): 45 calories, 0.5g fat, 118mg sodium, 9g carbs, 0.5g fiber, 4.5g sugars, 1.5g protein

Fruit-flavored fondue!?! Heck, yeah! This dip is sweet, creamy, and delicious.

Ingredients

1½ cups frozen peach slices
½ cup sugar-free pancake syrup
¼ cup fat-free cream cheese, room temperature
2 teaspoons light whipped butter or light buttery spread
1 tablespoon brown sugar (not packed)
1 tablespoon cornstarch
½ teaspoon vanilla extract
¼ teaspoon cinnamon
Dash salt

Directions

In a microwave-safe bowl, combine peaches and pancake syrup. Microwave for 1 minute.

Place peach mixture in a blender with cream cheese, and then blend until completely smooth. Set aside.

In a small bowl, combine cornstarch with 1 tablespoon cold water. Stir until cornstarch has dissolved. Add brown sugar, vanilla extract, cinnamon, and salt, stirring until mixed thoroughly.

Bring a medium pot to low heat and add butter. As butter begins to melt, add peach mixture and cornstarch mixture, and stir well.

Raise heat to medium-high. Stir continuously for 3 to 4 minutes, until mixture begins to bubble and thicken. Reduce heat to low, and allow mixture to return to a warm temperature.

If you have a fondue pot, transfer mixture to the pot and set temperature to low. If not, transfer to a bowl and dip away!

MAKES 7 SERVINGS

> **HG Tip!** This dip can be made in advance and re-heated to serve later. Heat over low heat so fondue does not burn.

Gooey Cinnamon Rolls with Cream Cheese Icing, p. 36

Morning Minis

Slammin' Smoked Salmon 'n Bacon B-Fast Sandwich, p. 13

Fro-Yo'ed Up Oatmeal Sundae, p. 34

Tutti Frutti Biscuits, p. 14

Easy Caprese Breakfast Pizzas, p. 28

Piña Colada Parfait Surprise, p. 31

Cheesy-Good Breakfast Tartlets, p. 22

Cinnamon-Vanilla French Toast Nuggets, p. 21

Grab 'n Go Breakfast Cookies, p. 18

Egg-stravaganza

That's a Lotta Frittata, p. 44

Cheesed-Up Pepperoni Pizza Scramble, p. 46

Super-Cheesy All-American Breakfast Bake, p. 56

Scoopable Salads

I Can't Believe It's Not Potato Salad!, p. 72

Veggie-Loaded Tangy Tuna Salad, p. 65

Sweet 'n Chunky Chicken Salad, p. 68

Start Me Up!

Sassy Southwestern Egg Rolls, p. 94

Mmmm-azing Mini Mushroom Tartlets, p. 100

Devilish Eggs, p. 104

H-O-T Hot Boneless Buffalo Wings, p. 88

Bacon-Bundled BBQ Shrimp, p. 85

Nacho-Average Tortilla Chips, p. 129

Sweet Caramelized Onion Dip, p. 122

Holy Moly Guacamole, p. 112

Scoopable Chinese Chicken Salad, p. 77

fluffy speckled peanut butter dip

PER SERVING (2 heaping tablespoons): 49 calories, 1.5g fat, 64mg sodium, 7.5g carbs, <0.5g fiber, 2g sugars, 0.5g protein

We've dipped apple slices, strawberries, pretzel sticks, and even celery stalks into this stuff (yes, it's true). Of course a plain old spoon works, too.

Ingredients

1 Jell-O Sugar Free Vanilla Pudding Snack

¾ cup Cool Whip Free, thawed

¼ cup Reese's Puffs cereal (original)

1 tablespoon reduced-fat peanut butter, room temperature

¼ teaspoon vanilla extract

1 no-calorie sweetener packet

Directions

Place cereal in a sealable plastic bag. Using a rolling pin or a can, crush cereal completely by rolling it firmly over the bag on a flat surface. Set aside.

In a bowl, combine pudding and peanut butter, stirring until completely mixed.

Add Cool Whip, vanilla extract, and sweetener, stirring until mixed well.

Stir in cereal crumbs and place bowl in the fridge. Refrigerate for at least 10 minutes before serving. Enjoy!

MAKES 6 SERVINGS

very-veggie spread

PER SERVING (⅓ cup): 45 calories, 1.25g fat, 244mg sodium, 6.5g carbs, 2.5g fiber, 2g sugars, 2g protein

This is called a spread, but it's definitely good enough to eat as a snack or side dish. Veggie-tastic!

Ingredients

1 medium eggplant, ends removed

2 cups roughly chopped fresh spinach leaves

1½ cups chopped portabello mushrooms

¾ cup canned cannellini beans, drained

One 14.5-ounce can diced tomatoes with roasted garlic, drained thoroughly

1 tablespoon olive oil

½ teaspoon salt, divided

¼ teaspoon crushed garlic

Optional: additional salt, black pepper

Directions

Peel eggplant carefully. Cut into ½-inch-thick circles. Salt lightly on both sides, using about ⅛ teaspoon of the salt total.

Spray a large pan with nonstick spray and bring to medium-high heat. Cook eggplant slices for 4 to 5 minutes on each side, pressing down with a spatula occasionally, until soft. Set aside to cool.

Remove pan from heat and re-spray with nonstick spray. Return to medium-high heat. Add mushrooms and cook for 2 minutes, stirring occasionally.

Add spinach to the pan and toss and cook until wilted. Drain excess liquid and set aside to cool.

Place beans, olive oil, and 1 tablespoon water in a blender or food processor. Puree until smooth. If blending slows, stop blender, remove from base, push mixture down toward the blade, and then continue blending.

Place eggplant in a large bowl and roughly mash with a potato masher or fork.

Add bean mixture, veggie mixture, canned tomatoes, ¼ teaspoon plus ⅛ teaspoon salt, and crushed garlic to the bowl. Mix well to combine.

Let sit, at room temperature or in the fridge, for at least 1 hour to allow flavors to combine. If you like, season to taste with pepper and additional salt. Enjoy hot, warm, or cold!

MAKES 12 SERVINGS

HG Tip! This one tastes better the longer it sits.

Big Dippers!

Wondering what else you can dip into some of your dippy new pals? Check out these ideas . . .

❋ **Toasty and Tasty:** Make mini toasts out of wheat bread. Using a serrated knife, carefully cut a thick piece of whole-wheat bread into two thin slices. Then cut each slice into four squares. Bake in the oven at 350 degrees for 3 to 4 minutes. Eight mini toasts contain around 100 calories! Recommended dips: Crazy-Creamy Spinach Artichoke Dip and Hungry, Hungry Artichoke Hummus.

❋ **Saved by the Bell:** Slice red bell peppers (those are the sweetest) into little bite-sized "boats." They're perfect little dip-holders. Recommended dips: Sweet Caramelized Onion Dip, Mexican Bean & Cheese Dip, Very-Veggie Spread.

❋ **Protein-Packed and Ready for Action:** Attention, meat-lovers! Skewer some chicken, lean beef, or shrimp, and grill or bake until fully cooked. Then dip away! Recommended dips: Kickin' Peanut Sauce, Holy Moly Guacamole, Not-So-Secret BBQ Sauce.

❋ **100-Calorie Dippers . . . Sweet!:** Portion-controlled packs of mini cookies come in a zillion varieties and are PERFECT to dip into any of our sweet, desserty dips. Go crazy! Recommended dips: Chunky Caramel-Apple Pumpkin Dip, Creamy Vanilla Dip, Fluffy Speckled Peanut Butter Dip, Fluffy Cinnamon–Cream Cheese Dip.

chapter six

mini meal mania

Bitty Bites with Bigtime Flavor

Wondering what exactly a "mini meal" is? It's something so satisfying that you could consider it a meal, but with few enough calories that you could eat many of 'em throughout the day. That's actually the best thing about the little meals in this chapter—the calorie counts are so reasonable that these can double as super-filling snacks. Who wants a boring energy bar when you could have one of these?

totally pumpin' fettuccine

PER SERVING (entire recipe): 129 calories, 3g fat, 639mg sodium, 19g carbs, 6.5g fiber, 6g sugars, 7g protein

It's pumpkin time again, peeps! This recipe is for noodles surrounded by a rich, creamy, DELICIOUS, pumpkin-infused sauce. Yum ...

Ingredients

1 package House Foods Tofu Shirataki Fettuccine Shaped Noodle Substitute
One-half wedge The Laughing Cow Light Original Swiss cheese
¼ cup plain light soymilk
¼ cup canned pure pumpkin
¼ cup fat-free chicken broth
¼ cup finely chopped onion
1 teaspoon reduced-fat Parmesan-style grated topping
½ teaspoon chopped garlic
½ teaspoon garlic powder
⅛ teaspoon salt
Dash black pepper
Optional: additional salt and
     black pepper

Directions

Rinse and drain shirataki noodles well. Pat dry. Place noodles in a microwave-safe bowl and microwave for 1 minute.

Drain excess liquid from noodles. Dry noodles thoroughly, using paper towels to soak up as much moisture as possible. Cut noodles up a bit using a knife or kitchen shears. Set aside.

In a separate dish, combine soymilk, pumpkin, garlic powder, salt, and pepper. Mix well and set aside.

Bring a small saucepan to high heat. Add chicken broth, onion, garlic, and cheese wedge half. Stirring occasionally to break up the cheese, cook until broth has mostly evaporated, 2 to 4 minutes.

Reduce heat to medium and continue to cook for just 1 minute or so, until onion and garlic begin to brown. Add pumpkin mixture. Stir until sauce is thoroughly blended and hot.

Add sauce to your noodles and stir well. If you like, season to taste with more salt and pepper. Finish with Parm-style topping and enjoy!

MAKES 1 SERVING

HG Tip! Find House Foods Tofu Shirataki at select supermarkets, most Whole Foods locations, and Japanese markets.

ez tomato-basil chicken

PER SERVING (¼th of recipe): 175 calories, 1.5g fat,
251mg sodium, 11g carbs, 2g fiber, 6g sugars, 28g protein

It really is EASY. Three ingredients, peeps! It's also extremely DELICIOUS!

Ingredients

1 pound raw boneless skinless lean chicken breast tenders
1½ cups (half a 28-ounce can) crushed tomatoes with basil
1½ cups thinly sliced onions

Directions

Preheat oven to 350 degrees.

Bring a pan sprayed with nonstick spray to high heat on the stove. Add onions and cook just until they begin to brown, about 3 minutes.

Pour half the tomatoes (one-fourth of the can) into a medium baking pan. Lay chicken in the pan and top with onions.

Pour the rest of the tomatoes (another one-fourth of the can) evenly over chicken and onion. Bake in the oven for about 30 minutes, until chicken is cooked through.

Allow chicken to cool and sauce to thicken slightly before serving. Ta-da!

MAKES 4 SERVINGS

For Weight Watchers *POINTS*®
values and photos of all the
recipes in this book, check out
hungry-girl.com/book.

crazy calypso salad

PER SERVING (about 2 cups): 174 calories, 5g fat, 429mg sodium, 21.5g carbs, 4g fiber, 13.5g sugars, 12g protein

This salad has shrimp, mango, avocado, and a sweet citrus dressing. It's like a tropical vacation in your salad bowl!

Ingredients

For Salad
8 cups fresh spinach leaves
8 ounces cooked medium shrimp
2 cups chopped mango (about 2 mangos)
1 cup cubed avocado (about 1 small avocado)

For Dressing
⅓ cup seasoned rice vinegar
2 tablespoons lime juice
1 no-calorie sweetener packet
⅛ teaspoon cayenne pepper

Directions

Combine all ingredients for dressing in a small bowl. Mix well and set aside.

In a large serving bowl, combine all salad ingredients. Pour dressing over salad. Toss until all ingredients are coated. Devour!

MAKES 5 SERVINGS

 For a pic of this recipe, see the second photo insert. Yay!

big bad burger wrap

PER SERVING (entire recipe): 199 calories, 5.5g fat,
1,368mg sodium, 27.5g carbs, 16.5g fiber, 4.5g sugars, 23.5g protein

This is a HUGE hit with guys. Maybe it's because the mix of mustard, ketchup, and pickles makes it taste EXACTLY like fast food . . . Yeah, that must be it.

Ingredients

1 large La Tortilla Factory Smart & Delicious Low Carb/High Fiber tortilla
1 Boca Original Meatless Burger
1 wedge The Laughing Cow Light Original Swiss cheese
1 pickle spear, chopped
1 teaspoon mustard
1 teaspoon ketchup
2 dashes Frank's RedHot Original Cayenne Pepper Sauce

Directions

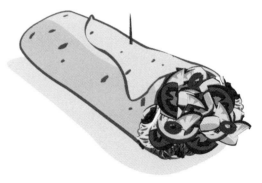

Prepare Boca patty according to box directions, either in the microwave or in a pan sprayed with nonstick spray. Chop patty into bite-sized pieces. Set aside.

To make sauce, combine mustard, ketchup, and hot sauce in a small dish. Stir well and set aside.

Warm tortilla in the microwave for 10 seconds. Lay tortilla flat and spread cheese wedge on top.

Place chopped burger and pickle in the center of the tortilla. Top with sauce. Fold the sides of the tortilla in, and then roll it up from the bottom. Enjoy!

MAKES 1 SERVING

smothered pig in a blanket

PER SERVING (entire recipe): 196 calories, 5.25g fat, 950mg sodium, 24g carbs, 2.5g fiber, 5g sugars, 14g protein

Our guilt-free piggies in a blanket (find those in our first book) have been such a hit, we decided to take that recipe to the next level. This time it's super-sized and smothered . . .

Ingredients

1 fat-free (or nearly fat-free) hot dog

1 serving Pillsbury Reduced Fat Crescent Rolls refrigerated dough

½ slice fat-free cheddar cheese (cut slice on a diagonal so your half is triangle-shaped)

¼ cup low-fat veggie chili

Directions

Preheat oven to 375 degrees.

Stretch or roll out the triangle-shaped dough slightly, to make it a larger triangle.

Lay cheese triangle at the base of the dough. Place hot dog at the base and gently roll it up.

Place your blanketed pup in a baking pan sprayed lightly with nonstick spray. Bake in the oven for 12 to 14 minutes, until dough appears slightly browned and crispy.

Meanwhile, heat chili in the microwave. Once your pig in a blanket is fully cooked, plate it and top with chili.

MAKES 1 SERVING

 For a pic of this recipe, see the second photo insert. Yay!

HG Fast Fact:

Other names for the ever-popular Pigs in a Blanket include "Wiener Winks," "Kilted Sausages," and "*Würstchen im Schlafrock*," which pretty much means "sausage in a nightgown." Oooooh, pretty!!!

so low mein with chicken

PER SERVING (1½ cups): 167 calories, 1.5g fat, 925mg sodium, 19g carbs, 6g fiber, 4g sugars, 18g protein

I crave chicken lo mein but avoid it at all costs, since it has astronomically high fat and calorie counts. This version tastes as good as regular lo mein (yes, AS GOOD!) but has a teeny-tiny fraction of the calories and fat. This recipe's a Keeper, people!

Ingredients

3 packages House Foods Tofu Shirataki Spaghetti Shaped Noodle Substitute

One bag (about 12 ounces) frozen Chinese-style stir-fry mixed veggies

8 ounces raw boneless skinless lean chicken breast, cut into strips

1 cup bean sprouts

½ cup chopped mushrooms

½ cup thinly sliced zucchini

½ cup chopped scallions

¼ cup shredded carrots

¼ cup reduced-sodium or light soy sauce

1 tablespoon cornstarch

2 teaspoons chicken-flavored powdered consommé

2 no-calorie sweetener packets

Directions

Rinse and drain shirataki noodles well. Dry noodles thoroughly, using paper towels to soak up as much moisture as possible. Use a knife or kitchen shears to slice them up a bit. Set aside.

To make sauce, combine soy sauce, cornstarch, consommé, and sweetener with ½ cup hot water. Stir well and set aside.

Bring a large pan or a wok sprayed with nonstick spray to medium-high heat. Add frozen veggies, chicken, bean sprouts, mushrooms, zucchini, scallions, and carrots. Sauté for 5 to 7 minutes, stirring frequently, until chicken is cooked through and frozen veggies are thawed and hot. Pour sauce into the pan or wok. Stir well and continue to cook until sauce has thickened, about 3 to 4 minutes.

Add noodles and cook, stirring occasionally, until entire dish is thoroughly mixed and hot. Serve it up and enjoy!!

MAKES 4 SERVINGS

 For a pic of this recipe, see the second photo insert. Yay!

HG Alternative!

Try this recipe with any lean protein. It's great with shrimp, tofu, or lean pork. Yum!

bbq mango tilapia

PER SERVING (½ of recipe): 197 calories, 2.5g fat,
500mg sodium, 18g carbs, 1g fiber, 15g sugars, 26.5g protein

Tilapia is one of my favorite fishes. Mango is one of my favorite fruits.
And BBQ is one of my favorite sauces. I LOVE THIS DISH!

Ingredients

Two 4.5-ounce fillets raw tilapia

¼ cup canned diced tomatoes, drained

¼ cup diced mango

¼ cup canned tomato sauce

2 tablespoons mango nectar

2 tablespoons ketchup

2 teaspoons brown sugar (not packed)

2 teaspoons cider vinegar

1 teaspoon molasses

½ teaspoon garlic powder

Directions

In a medium bowl, combine tomato sauce, mango nectar, ketchup, brown sugar, vinegar, molasses, and garlic powder. Mix well, and then stir in diced tomatoes and mango.

Place fish and sauce in a container and toss to coat.

Cover and let marinate in the fridge for 30 minutes.

Preheat oven to 375 degrees.

Spray a medium oven-safe baking dish with nonstick spray. Transfer sauce and fish to the dish. Cook for 10 to 15 minutes, until fish is cooked through.

Plate tilapia and top with any excess sauce. Enjoy!

MAKES 2 SERVINGS

For a pic of this recipe, see the second photo insert. Yay!

HG Trivia Tidbit:

One of the healthiest things about tilapia—they're herbivores. This means they consume fewer toxins than the fish-eat-fish types and are safer for us to eat. Tilapia is also now the 5th most commonly eaten seafood in the U.S.

For Weight Watchers *POINTS*® values and photos of all the recipes in this book, check out hungry-girl.com/book.

chicken fajita lettuce cups

PER SERVING (3 lettuce cups): 190 calories, 2.5g fat, 562mg sodium, 18g carbs, 4g fiber, 7g sugars, 23g protein

No tortillas needed for these fajitas! They work FANTASTICALLY well in little lettuce cups . . . and that saves you lots of calories.

Ingredients

3 leaves romaine, butter, or green leaf lettuce

3 ounces raw boneless skinless lean chicken breast, sliced

½ cup sliced red and green bell peppers

½ cup sliced onions

2 tablespoons Holy Moly Guacamole (page 112)

1 tablespoon salsa

1 tablespoon fat-free sour cream

1½ teaspoons dry fajita seasoning mix

Directions

Place chicken, peppers, and onions in a medium bowl. In a separate dish, blend fajita seasoning mix with 3 tablespoons water.

Pour seasoning mixture over chicken and veggies. Stir until chicken and veggies are thoroughly coated. Let marinate for 5 minutes.

Spray a medium pan with nonstick spray and bring to medium-high heat. Pour chicken-veggie mixture—including any excess marinade—into the pan.

Stirring occasionally, sauté until chicken is cooked through and veggies are slightly browned, about 6 minutes. Transfer mixture to a bowl.

Enjoy fajita-style, by loading up each lettuce "cup" with one-third of the chicken-veggie mixture and topping with the guacamole, salsa, and sour cream. Yum!

MAKES 1 SERVING

📷 For a pic of this recipe, see the second photo insert. Yay!

HG Alternative!

Don't feel like whipping up a batch of HG's guacamole? No worries. You can use store-bought guac instead. Then the entire recipe will have around 213 calories, 6 grams fat, 17.5 grams carbs, and 2.5 grams fiber. Not bad!

Chew on This

The word "fajita" is the diminutive form of the Spanish word *"faja,"* meaning "belt" or "girdle." Small belt? That's how we like 'em! Make your fajitas like this and your *faja* will hopefully stay, um, *ita*.

crazy-good coconut chicken taco

PER SERVING (1 taco): 198 calories, 2.25g fat, 466mg sodium, 21g carbs, 3.75g fiber, 7g sugars, 22.5g protein

You'll feel like a fancy little chef, making your own taco shell and all. But this tropical taco recipe is really easy to throw together, and it is VERY unique.

Ingredients

3 ounces raw boneless skinless lean chicken breast, cut into strips

1 medium corn tortilla

½ cup sliced red bell pepper

¼ cup sugar-free calorie-free coconut syrup

2 tablespoons pineapple salsa

½ tablespoon fat-free sour cream

½ teaspoon garlic powder

⅛ teaspoon salt

Directions

Preheat oven to 400 degrees.

Once oven is hot, use tongs to carefully drape tortilla over two grates in the oven rack, so that the tortilla hangs from the rack. Bake for about 5 minutes, or until tortilla forms a firm taco shell. (Shell will harden completely after cooling.) Use tongs to carefully remove the shell, then let cool.

Place coconut syrup, garlic powder, and salt in a medium pot. Add ½ cup water and mix well. Add chicken and pepper slices to the pot and bring to low heat on the stove.

Cook until chicken is thoroughly cooked and tender, stirring occasionally, about 15 minutes. Remove pot from heat and drain liquid completely.

Place chicken and bell pepper in the taco shell. Top with salsa and sour cream. Taco time!!

MAKES 1 SERVING

 For a pic of this recipe, see the second photo insert. Yay!

HG Alternatives!

Having a hard time locating calorie-free coconut syrup? Instead just add an extra ¼ cup water, 1 teaspoon coconut extract, and 1 tablespoon Splenda No Calorie Sweetener (granulated). And if you can't find pineapple salsa, stir some canned pineapple tidbits (in juice) into some regular salsa.

turkey-tastic creamy shirataki bowls

This mini meal is filling, creamy, and delicious. It tastes like something FATTENING-yet-FANTASTIC your mom would make.

Ingredients

1 pound raw extra-lean ground turkey

2 packages House Foods Tofu Shirataki Spaghetti Shaped Noodle Substitute

One 8-ounce can sliced water chestnuts, drained

One 10.75-ounce can 98 percent fat-free cream of mushroom condensed soup

1 wedge The Laughing Cow Light Original Swiss cheese, room temperature

3 cups broccoli florets

1 cup fat-free chicken or vegetable broth

1 cup shredded carrots

6 tablespoons fat-free sour cream

½ cup chopped scallions

2 tablespoons dry onion soup/dip seasoning mix

½ teaspoon garlic powder

¼ teaspoon seasoned salt

¼ teaspoon black pepper

Directions

Rinse and drain shirataki noodles well. Dry noodles thoroughly, using paper towels to soak up as much moisture as possible. Use a knife or kitchen shears to slice them up a bit. Set aside.

To prepare sauce, combine mushroom soup with ¼ cup water, cheese wedge, and sour cream, stirring until mixed thoroughly. Set aside.

Place turkey in a large bowl. Sprinkle with seasoned salt, black pepper, and garlic powder. Mix well to distribute spices.

In a small dish, combine onion seasoning mix with ½ cup water. Stir thoroughly.

Spray a large pan with nonstick spray and bring to medium heat. Add seasoned turkey and the onion seasoning mixture. Use a wooden spoon to break up the turkey. Cook until liquid has been mostly absorbed and turkey is fully browned, about 15 minutes. Then transfer turkey to another large bowl.

Remove pan from heat, and re-spray with nonstick spray. Over medium heat, add noodles, broccoli, broth, carrots, and water chestnuts. Stir until entire dish is hot.

Return turkey to the pan. Continue cooking, stirring frequently, until vegetables have softened, 7 to 8 minutes. Add scallions and sauce and stir. Continue to cook for 1 additional minute, or until sauce is evenly distributed and hot.

Serve each portion in a bowl and top with a tablespoon of sour cream. Enjoy!

MAKES 6 SERVINGS

> **HG Tip!** Find House Foods Tofu Shirataki at select supermarkets, most Whole Foods locations, and Japanese markets.

super veggie-stuffed peppers

PER SERVING (2 stuffed-pepper halves): 188 calories, 2g fat, 801mg sodium, 28.5g carbs, 8.5g fiber, 13.5g sugars, 19g protein

These are large and in charge! They can be center-plate entrées served with sides OR side dishes themselves. What CAN'T these talented, overgrown, vegetable-packed peppers do?!

Ingredients

1 large red bell pepper

1 plum tomato (preferably Roma), deseeded and chopped

½ cup frozen ground-beef-style soy crumbles, thawed

½ cup chopped mushrooms

¼ cup chopped onion

¼ cup chopped green bell pepper

¼ cup canned tomato sauce

2 tablespoons shredded fat-free cheddar cheese

½ teaspoon dry taco seasoning mix

¼ teaspoon minced garlic

Directions

Preheat oven to 375 degrees.

Bring a medium pan to medium-high heat on the stove. Add mushrooms, onion, and green bell pepper. Cook for 3 to 5 minutes, stirring occasionally, until veggies are slightly softened. Add garlic to the pan and cook for 1 additional minute. Transfer mixture to a medium bowl.

To the bowl, add tomato, soy crumbles, tomato sauce, cheese, and taco seasoning mix. Mix thoroughly and set aside.

Slice off the top of the red pepper, and then slice it in half lengthwise. Remove seeds.

Spray a medium baking dish lightly with nonstick spray. Place pepper halves in the dish, cut side up, and bake in the oven for 25 minutes.

Remove pepper halves from the oven and reduce temperature to 350 degrees.

Once pepper halves are cool enough to handle, use paper towels to soak up any excess moisture. Evenly spoon veggie mixture into pepper halves. Return to the oven and bake for 20 minutes. Let cool slightly and then dig in!

MAKES 1 SERVING

For Weight Watchers *POINTS*®
values and photos of all the
recipes in this book, check out
hungry-girl.com/book.

blc wraps

PER SERVING (3 lettuce wraps): 163 calories, 1.5g fat, 1,182mg sodium, 18g carbs, 5.5g fiber, 8g sugars, 21.5g protein

Bacon, lettuce, cheeseburger. Woohoo!

Ingredients

3 leaves romaine, butter, or green leaf lettuce

1 Boca Original Meatless Burger

1 slice extra-lean turkey bacon

1 slice fat-free cheddar cheese

2 tablespoons chopped tomato

1 tablespoon chopped onion

2 dill pickle slices, chopped

1 tablespoon ketchup

1 tablespoon fat-free mayonnaise

Directions

Cook burger patty according to package instructions, either in the microwave or in a pan sprayed with nonstick spray.

Top burger with the cheese slice. Microwave for about 20 seconds, until cheese melts. Set aside.

Cook bacon slice in a pan sprayed with nonstick spray, until both sides are crispy.

Once burger and bacon are cool enough to handle, chop both into bite-sized pieces.

Place burger and bacon pieces in a small bowl. Add tomato, onion, and pickles, and mix well. Add ketchup and mayo. Toss to coat.

Put one-third of the burger mixture into each lettuce "cup" and dig in!

MAKES 1 SERVING

philly cheesesteak lettuce cups

PER SERVING (2 lettuce cups): 197 calories, 7.5g fat,
345mg sodium, 7g carbs, 1g fiber, 4g sugars, 23.5g protein

We're kicking unwanted calories and carbs to the curb here by serving up our cheesesteak in lettuce cups instead of on a giant doughy roll. Who's smart? WE ARE!

Ingredients

2 leaves romaine, butter, or green leaf lettuce
3 ounces raw lean beefsteak fillet
⅓ cup sliced mushrooms
¼ cup thinly sliced onions
1 slice fat-free American cheese

Directions

Slice your fillet into thin strips.

Spray a medium pan with nonstick spray and bring to medium-high heat. Add mushrooms and onions. Cook for about 5 minutes, stirring occasionally, until onions are slightly browned. Transfer veggies to a bowl and set aside.

Remove pan from heat, and re-spritz with nonstick spray. Cook fillet strips over medium-high heat for 1 to 2 minutes, flipping them halfway through cooking.

Break cheese slice into small strips. Place cheese on top of meat—still in the pan—and continue to cook until cheese has melted slightly.

Remove from heat and mix the cheesy beef strips in with the veggies. Serve in lettuce "cups."

MAKES 1 SERVING

 For a pic of this recipe, see the second photo insert. Yay!

HG Tip! Freezing your beef slightly will make it easier to cut.

chicken fajita pita

PER SERVING (entire recipe): 180 calories, 1.5g fat, 364mg sodium, 18.5g carbs, 3.5g fiber, 2.5g sugars, 22.5g protein

WOW! A fajita-stuffed pita for under 200 calories. VERY impressive!

Ingredients

3 ounces raw boneless skinless lean chicken breast, cut into strips

One-half whole-wheat or high-fiber pita

¼ cup sliced green bell pepper

¼ cup sliced onions

1 small lettuce leaf

1 teaspoon dry fajita seasoning mix

Optional toppings: salsa, fat-free sour cream

Directions

In a small bowl, combine fajita seasoning with 1 tablespoon water, until mixed well.

Add chicken, green pepper, and onions to the bowl, and stir to coat evenly with seasoning mixture. Place bowl in the fridge to marinate for at least 30 minutes.

Once marinated, bring a medium pan sprayed with nonstick spray to medium-high heat. Add contents of bowl, including any excess marinade, to the pan. Sauté until chicken is cooked through, stirring frequently, 5 to 7 minutes.

Place lettuce leaf inside the pita, and then fill pita with chicken-and-veggie mixture. Add some salsa and/or sour cream, if you like.

MAKES 1 SERVING

superb-y herby sauce-exposed pizzas

> PER SERVING (entire recipe): 144 calories, 2.75g fat, 625mg sodium, 24g carbs, 6g fiber, 2g sugars, 8.5g protein

Sometimes the sauce wants the spotlight . . .

▭ Ingredients

1 light English muffin

1 wedge The Laughing Cow Light Garlic & Herb cheese

2 tablespoons canned tomato sauce with Italian seasonings

Optional toppings: dried Italian seasonings (basil, oregano, etc.)

▭ Directions

Split English muffin in half. Toast for about 5 minutes, until crispy.

Spread cheese wedge evenly over both halves. Spread sauce over the cheese.

Now toast your cheesed 'n sauced English muffin for about 2 minutes, until cheese has melted and sauce is warm.

If you like, season the tops as you would a regular slice of pizza. Now chew!

MAKES 1 SERVING

HG Tip! These are best made in a toaster oven. Don't have one? Toast the muffin in a regular toaster. Once covered with cheese and sauce, pop 'em in the oven at 450 degrees for a few minutes.

cheesy saucy veggie stacks

Veggies. Sauce. Cheese. And more veggies. They're like cute little veggie napoleons . . . only they're HUGE, not little! These are still cute though, so no worries.

Ingredients

1 large portabello mushroom, sliced into ½-inch-wide strips

1 medium eggplant, ends removed

2 small zucchinis

1 cup canned tomato sauce with Italian seasonings

½ cup canned spinach, drained and thoroughly patted dry

½ cup fat-free ricotta cheese

2 tablespoons chopped basil

1 teaspoon reduced-fat Parmesan-style grated topping

1 teaspoon dried minced onion

⅛ teaspoon salt

¼ teaspoon garlic powder

Dash nutmeg

Directions

Preheat oven to 425 degrees.

Slice eggplant in half lengthwise. Cut each half lengthwise into three slices. Cut off rounded sides of the two outer slices, so that all slices are flat on both sides.

Cut zucchini on a diagonal into ½-inch-wide slices. Discard the ends.

Set out a few layers of paper towels. As you cook veggies in the next few steps, transfer them to the paper towels to drain excess moisture.

Spray a large pan evenly with nonstick spray and bring to medium-high heat on the stove.

Lay zucchini slices flat in the pan and cook for 3 minutes per side. Remove from pan and place on paper towels.

Remove pan from heat and re-spray. Cook mushroom slices for 2 minutes per side. Remove from pan and place on paper towels.

Remove pan from heat and re-spray. Cook eggplant slices for 3 minutes per side. Remove from pan and place on paper towels.

In a small dish, combine spinach, ricotta cheese, basil, minced onion, salt, garlic powder, and nutmeg. Stir well and set aside.

Spray a deep oven-safe pan with nonstick spray. Place half of the tomato sauce in the center of the pan, and place two eggplant slices side by side over the sauce, leaving an inch or so between them. These slices are the bases for the two "stacks."

Spread about one-fourth of the spinach mixture on top of each slice. Then layer about one-fourth of the zucchini and mushroom slices on top of each stack. Over each veggie layer, add another eggplant slice.

Spread the rest of the spinach mixture on top of stacks. Layer remaining zucchini and mushroom slices.

Cover stacks with remaining eggplant slices. Finish it all off with the rest of the tomato sauce and the Parm-style topping.

Bake in the oven for 25 minutes.

MAKES 2 SERVINGS

📷 For a pic of this recipe, see the second photo insert. Yay!

For Weight Watchers *POINTS*®
values and photos of all the
recipes in this book, check out
hungry-girl.com/book.

dan's snazzy green pepper pizzas

PER SERVING (3 pieces): 189 calories, 3.25g fat, 1,312mg sodium, 19.5g carbs, 4g fiber, 7g sugars, 18.5g protein

Using green peppers as pizza crust is a GREAT way to save calories and carbs. That idea came from my husband, Dan (the genius behind Dan Good Chili, which can be found in the first HG book). Thanks, Sweetie!

Ingredients

2 large green bell peppers

¾ cup shredded fat-free mozzarella cheese

17 pieces turkey pepperoni, chopped

One 8-ounce can (about 1 cup) tomato sauce with Italian seasonings

¼ cup chopped mushrooms

3 tablespoons chopped red onion

One-half no-calorie sweetener packet

1 tablespoon reduced-fat Parmesan-style grated topping

Salt, black pepper, onion powder, garlic powder, to taste

Directions

Preheat oven to 350 degrees.

Cut each pepper lengthwise into thirds, so you have six "boat"-shaped pieces. Discard stems and seeds.

Place pepper pieces on a baking sheet sprayed with nonstick spray. Bake in the oven for 25 to 30 minutes, until peppers are slightly soft and edges look cooked.

Meanwhile, in a medium bowl, mix tomato sauce with sweetener. Season to taste with salt, black pepper, onion powder, and garlic powder. Stir in mushrooms and onion.

Once peppers are done, remove from the oven and set aside. Leave oven on. Once cool enough to handle, blot any excess moisture from inside the pepper pieces.

Evenly distribute veggie-sauce mixture among pepper "crusts," about 2 tablespoons for each pizza. Top with chopped pepperoni.

Evenly distribute mozzarella cheese among the pizzas. Bake in the oven for 10 minutes, until cheese has melted.

Remove pepper pizzas from the oven and top each with ½ teaspoon Parm-style topping. Let cool slightly. Now CHEW!

MAKES 2 SERVINGS

Chew on This

Ever wonder why bell peppers aren't hot like other peppers? Bell peppers actually have a recessive gene that cuts out capsaicin, the stuff that makes other peppers spicy. Learning is fun . . . Weeeee!

fettuccine hungry girlfredo veggie explosion

PER SERVING (entire recipe): 151 calories, 4.5g fat, 407mg sodium, 20g carbs, 7g fiber, 7g sugars, 9g protein

This Fettuccine Hungry Girlfredo has been attacked by veggies . . . and it's gooooooooood!

Ingredients

1 package House Foods Tofu Shirataki Fettuccine Shaped Noodle Substitute

1 wedge The Laughing Cow Light Original Swiss cheese, room temperature

½ cup small broccoli florets

½ cup red bell pepper chunks

½ cup zucchini chunks

1 tablespoon fat-free sour cream

2 teaspoons reduced-fat Parmesan-style grated topping

Salt and black pepper, to taste

Optional: garlic powder, chili powder

Directions

Place all veggies in a medium microwave-safe bowl with 2 tablespoons water. Cover and microwave for 2 to 3 minutes, until veggies are tender. Once the bowl is cool enough to handle, drain water and set aside.

Rinse and drain shirataki noodles well. Dry noodles thoroughly, using paper towels to soak up as much moisture as possible. Use a knife or kitchen shears to slice them up a bit.

Place noodles in a microwave-safe bowl and top with sour cream and Parm-style topping. Break cheese wedge into pieces and add to the bowl. Microwave for 1 minute.

Stir well and microwave again for 1 minute.

Mix in veggies and season well with salt and pepper. Add some garlic powder and/or chili powder, if you like. Enjoy!

MAKES 1 SERVING

HG Tip! Find House Foods Tofu Shirataki at select supermarkets, most Whole Foods locations, and Japanese markets.

mmm mmm goo-lash

PER SERVING (entire recipe): 197 calories, 5.75g fat, 1,258mg sodium, 20g carbs, 6.5g fiber, 3.5g sugars, 17.5g protein

This is ridiculously creamy, thanks to two types of cheese and cream of celery soup. Soy crumbles and veggies beef up this noodle dish. All in all, it's pretty spectacular (even though it may look a little scary).

Ingredients

1 package House Foods Tofu Shirataki Fettuccine Shaped Noodle Substitute

⅓ cup 98 percent fat-free cream of celery soup

⅓ cup frozen ground-beef-style soy crumbles

¼ cup chopped mushrooms

2 tablespoons chopped onion

1 slice fat-free American cheese

1 wedge The Laughing Cow Light Original Swiss cheese

Salt, to taste

Optional topping: fat-free sour cream

Directions

Rinse and drain shirataki noodles well. Pat dry. Place noodles in a microwave-safe bowl and microwave for 1 minute.

Drain excess liquid from noodles. Dry noodles thoroughly, using paper towels to soak up as much moisture as possible. Cut noodles up a bit using a knife or kitchen shears. Set aside.

Spray a medium pan with nonstick spray and bring to medium heat. Add onion and cook for 2 minutes. Add mushrooms to the pan. Continue to cook until onion is soft.

Add crumbles to the pan and cook for 1 additional minute, until crumbles are thawed and hot.

Add soup and stir to coat veggies and crumbles. Once hot, place American cheese slice on the mixture. As it melts—it will melt pretty quickly—go ahead and mix it into the sauce.

Break up cheese wedge and stir it into the "goo," making sure it separates and melts.

Reduce heat and add noodles to the pan. Stir to coat.

Transfer to your favorite bowl. Season to taste with salt and, if you like, add a dollop of sour cream. Mmmmm!

MAKES 1 SERVING

HG Fast Fact:

Goulash is a dish that originated in Hungary. We think it's only fitting that the latest variation comes from the Hungry Girl kitchen.

Snack Attack!

No time to whip up a mini meal? These supermarket finds will do the trick if you need a snack fix for under 200 calories.

✳ **Yoplait Light, Apple Turnover:** Here's to 100 calories of creamy, apple-tastic goodness! Fat-free yogurt is a great snack or dessert, and this one is amazing. And, if apple's not your thing, check out the other fun flavors—there's a slew of 'em! Fridge required.

✳ **98% Fat-Free Turkey Breast Slices:** Oscar Mayer, Sara Lee, and Applegate Farms all make great ones. They're low in calories, low in fat, and PACKED with protein. Fridge required.

✳ **Progresso Light Soup, Southwestern-Style Vegetable:** This soup is packed with flavor and fiber, yet it has just 60 calories and 0 grams fat per serving (and only about 120 calories for the whole can!). Fantastic! Microwave required.

✳ **94% Fat-Free Microwave Popcorn:** Jolly Time and Orville Redenbacher each make individual bags that have just 100 calories a bag. This stuff comes in fun flavors, too. Microwave required.

✳ **Amy's Mexican Tamale Pie:** Holy moly. This polenta-topped mini meal is AMAZING. And with just 150 calories and 3 grams fat, you can pretty much enjoy it whenever you get the urge. Freezer and microwave required.

✳ **Fiber One Toaster Pastries, Brown Sugar Cinnamon:** These are a Pop-Tart lover's dream. Each one's got 190 calories, 4 grams fat, and 5 whole grams of fiber. Fantastic! Toaster helpful but not required.

* chapter seven

tortilla madness

Quesadillas, Wraps, and So Much More

Sorry to get all Wikipedia on you, but did you know that the tortilla business is the fastest-growing sector in the U.S. baking industry? No surprise there—tortillas can be used instead of bread and dough to make guilt-free pizzas, sandwiches, wraps, and more. The reason the tortilla has become an HG staple is 'cuz we've found a version that is HUGE, contains only 80 calories, and has 12 whole grams of fiber. That makes it a nearly perfect food, especially for many of these low-cal recipes. If you can't locate our favorite—the large La Tortilla Factory Smart & Delicious Low Carb/High Fiber tortilla—no worries. Just look for any large, low-calorie, high-fiber one.

lean bean 'n cheese enchiladas

PER SERVING (1 enchilada): 187 calories, 2g fat, 976mg sodium, 29g carbs, 4g fiber, 5g sugars, 12g protein

These taste like authentic Mexican enchiladas—cheesy, beany, and soooooo yummy!

Ingredients

2 medium-large corn tortillas
⅔ cup enchilada sauce
⅓ cup fat-free refried beans
1 slice fat-free cheddar cheese, halved
¼ cup shredded fat-free cheddar cheese
¼ cup chopped onion
1 tablespoon taco sauce
½ teaspoon dry taco seasoning mix
Optional toppings: fat-free sour cream, chopped scallions

Directions

Preheat oven to 400 degrees.

In a pan sprayed with nonstick spray, cook onion over medium heat on the stove until it begins to brown, about 2 minutes.

In a small dish, combine onion with refried beans, taco sauce, and taco seasoning until mixed well.

Spray a small baking dish with nonstick spray and set aside.

Heat tortillas in the microwave until slightly warm. Lay tortillas flat and spread about 2 tablespoons enchilada sauce onto each one.

Place one half of the cheese slice in the center of each tortilla. Evenly distribute bean mixture in the center of each tortilla.

Wrap tortillas up tightly and place them in the baking dish, seam sides down. Pour the rest of the enchilada sauce over the enchiladas. Bake in the oven for about 10 minutes, until enchiladas are hot.

Remove dish from the oven and sprinkle shredded cheese over enchiladas. Return to the oven and bake for about 5 minutes, until cheese has melted.

Plate those babies and, if you like, top with sour cream and/or scallions.

MAKES 2 SERVINGS

HG Trivia Tidbit:

January 6th is National Bean Day. So, when that day rolls around, whip up a batch of these cheesy treats. We won't tell if you make them on other days, too!

For Weight Watchers **POINTS**®
values and photos of all the
recipes in this book, check out
hungry-girl.com/book.

turkey reuben quesadilla

PER SERVING (entire quesadilla): 186 calories, 6.5g fat, 1,104mg sodium, 25.5g carbs, 13g fiber, 4.5g sugars, 19g protein

If you're a fan of Reuben sandwiches, your head will explode when you try this crazy quesadilla. That's not a bad thing, folks.

○ Ingredients

1 large La Tortilla Factory Smart & Delicious Low Carb/High Fiber tortilla
1 ounce (about 2 slices) 98 percent fat-free turkey breast slices
1 slice reduced-fat Swiss cheese
2 tablespoons sauerkraut, drained
1 tablespoon fat-free Thousand Island dressing
Optional: additional sauerkraut

○ Directions

Cut cheese slice into four triangles. Set aside.

Lay tortilla flat and spread dressing over it, leaving about ½-inch of space around the perimeter. Arrange the cheese triangles on one half of the tortilla.

Spray a medium-large pan with nonstick spray and bring to medium heat. Place tortilla flat in the pan with the dressing-covered, cheese-topped side facing up.

Once cheese has begun to melt, top the cheese with turkey slices and sauerkraut, adding additional sauerkraut, if you like. Using a spatula, carefully fold the dressing-only half over the other half, pressing down lightly with the spatula to seal.

Continue cooking for about 1 minute, or until the bottom is slightly toasted. Flip tortilla and continue cooking for about 1 additional minute, or until desired level of toasty-ness is reached. Remove from heat, cut into four triangles, and enjoy!

MAKES 1 SERVING

Chew on This

Let's compare stats! Arby's Roast Turkey Reuben Sandwich has 594 calories, 30 grams fat, and 55 grams carbs. Now take a look at our quesadilla's nutritionals. Kinda makes you want to do a dance, doesn't it?

cheesy beefy quesadilla

PER SERVING (entire quesadilla): 196 calories, 5g fat, 931mg sodium, 25g carbs, 13.5g fiber, 2.5g sugars, 25.5g protein

Here's a little bit of Taco Bell magic, right in your very own kitchen. Unnecessary extra calories not included . . .

Ingredients

1 large La Tortilla Factory Smart & Delicious Low Carb/High Fiber tortilla
⅓ cup frozen ground-beef-style soy crumbles
¼ cup shredded fat-free cheddar cheese
One-half wedge The Laughing Cow Light Original Swiss cheese
1 tablespoon fat-free sour cream
½ tablespoon chopped scallions
¼ teaspoon dry taco seasoning mix
Optional: additional fat-free sour cream, for dipping

Directions

In a small microwave-safe bowl, combine soy crumbles, cheddar cheese, scallions, sour cream, and seasoning mix, stirring thoroughly. Microwave for 30 seconds. Give mixture another stir and set aside.

Lay tortilla flat and spread cheese wedge evenly over one half.

Bring a medium-large pan sprayed with nonstick spray to medium heat and lay tortilla in it with the cheesy side up. Cook for about 30 seconds.

Top the cheesy tortilla half with the soy crumble mixture.

Using a spatula, carefully fold the plain tortilla half over the other half, pressing down with the spatula to seal. Cook for about 1 minute, until slightly toasted on the bottom.

Flip and continue to cook for about 1 minute. The quesadilla is done when both sides are toasted. Remove from heat and cut into four triangles. Serve with sour cream for dipping, if you like.

MAKES 1 SERVING

HG Fast Fact:

¡Ay, caramba! Taco Bell's Steak Quesadilla has 520 calories and 28 grams fat! How do you say "shocker" in Spanish?!

For Weight Watchers **POINTS**®
values and photos of all the
recipes in this book, check out
hungry-girl.com/book.

blt quesadilla

PER SERVING (entire quesadilla): 175 calories, 4.5g fat, 1,026mg sodium, 26.5g carbs, 12.5g fiber, 7g sugars, 18.5g protein

A bacon, lettuce, and tomato quesadilla?! We'll stop at nothing to bring you the most creative and satisfying mini meals!

Ingredients

1 large La Tortilla Factory Smart & Delicious Low Carb/High Fiber tortilla
2 tablespoons fat-free shredded cheese (mozzarella or cheddar)
2 slices extra-lean turkey bacon
½ plum tomato (preferably Roma), diced
½ cup shredded lettuce
1 tablespoon fat-free mayonnaise
1 tablespoon ketchup

Directions

Cook bacon according to package directions, either in the microwave or in a pan sprayed with nonstick spray. Once cool enough to handle, roughly chop and set aside.

Bring a pan sprayed with nonstick spray to medium heat. Lay tortilla flat in the pan. Top evenly with cheese.

Once cheese begins to melt, cover half of the tortilla with bacon and tomato. Using a spatula, carefully fold the cheese-only side over the other half, pressing down with the spatula to seal. Cook for about 1 minute.

Flip and continue cooking for about 1 minute, or until both sides are toasty. Remove from heat.

To make the sauce, combine mayo and ketchup in a small dish. Cut quesadilla into triangles, top with the shredded lettuce and serve with sauce on the side.

MAKES 1 SERVING

buffalo chicken chop salad wrap

We took our famous Buffalo Chicken Choppity Chop (find that recipe in the salad chapter of the first HG book) and stuffed it inside a tortilla. Yeah, we're cool like that.

Ingredients

1 large La Tortilla Factory Smart & Delicious Low Carb/High Fiber tortilla
2½ ounces cooked skinless lean chicken breast, chopped
½ cup shredded lettuce
2½ teaspoons Frank's RedHot Original Cayenne Pepper Sauce
2 teaspoons reduced-fat Parmesan-style grated topping
1½ teaspoons fat-free sour cream

Directions

Place chicken pieces in a small microwave-safe dish. Top with hot sauce and Parm-style topping, and stir until chicken is thoroughly coated. Microwave for 45 seconds, or until hot.

Microwave tortilla until slightly warm. Lay tortilla flat and spread sour cream down the center. Place lettuce in the center of the tortilla, and top with chicken mixture.

Wrap tortilla up by folding in the sides first, and then rolling it up tightly from the bottom.

MAKES 1 SERVING

HG Alternative!

If you're a diehard fan of ranch or blue cheese dressing, try swapping the sour cream for a low-cal version of one of those!

crispy white pizza

PER SERVING (entire pizza): 176 calories, 3g fat, 947mg sodium, 29g carbs, 13g fiber, 7g sugars, 19g protein

Ahhhhhhhh! This guilt-free white pizza is so good, you will SCREAM when you take a bite. AHHHHHHHHHHHHHH!

Ingredients

1 large La Tortilla Factory Smart & Delicious Low Carb/High Fiber tortilla
⅓ cup fat-free ricotta cheese
¼ cup thinly sliced onions
1 tablespoon shredded fat-free mozzarella cheese
6 basil leaves
4 thin slices plum tomato (Romas rock)
¼ teaspoon garlic powder
⅛ teaspoon plus 1 dash salt
Dash black pepper

Directions

Preheat oven to 375 degrees.

Place tortilla on a baking sheet sprayed lightly with nonstick spray. Bake in the oven for 5 to 6 minutes on each side, until slightly crispy. Leave oven on.

In a small bowl, mix ricotta cheese, mozzarella cheese, garlic powder, ⅛ teaspoon salt, and black pepper. Set aside.

Bring a pan sprayed with nonstick spray to medium heat on the stove. Add onions and, stirring occasionally, cook until softened and slightly browned, about 3 minutes. Immediately stir onions into cheese mixture.

Spread cheese-onion mixture evenly on top of the tortilla. Place basil leaves on cheese-onion mixture. Top with tomato slices, and then sprinkle with a dash of salt.

Return pizza to the oven and bake for about 5 minutes, or until entire pizza is hot. Use a pizza cutter or a sharp knife to cut into slices. Pizza for one!

MAKES 1 SERVING

Chew on This

The world's most expensive pizza—dubbed "Pizza Royale 007"—was made with salmon, venison, lobster, caviar, and (holy moly!) edible gold. That crazy pie was auctioned off for 2,150 British pounds, and all the money went to charity.

spicy tortilla pizza mexicali

PER SERVING (entire pizza): 196 calories, 4g fat, 1,140mg sodium, 28.5g carbs, 14g fiber, 4g sugars, 24g protein

Here's another guilt-free pizza. This one has a little Mexican spin. Olé!

Ingredients

1 large La Tortilla Factory Smart & Delicious Low Carb/High Fiber tortilla

⅓ cup canned diced tomatoes with green chilies, drained

⅓ cup frozen ground-beef-style soy crumbles, thawed

2 tablespoons shredded fat-free cheddar cheese

2 tablespoons shredded fat-free mozzarella cheese

½ teaspoon dry taco seasoning mix

1 tablespoon fat-free sour cream

Directions

Preheat oven to 375 degrees.

Bring a medium-large pan sprayed lightly with nonstick spray to medium heat on the stove. Cook tortilla in the pan for a few minutes on each side until slightly firm.

Transfer tortilla to a baking sheet sprayed with nonstick spray. Spread tomatoes with chilies evenly over tortilla, leaving about 1 inch of space around the perimeter.

In a small dish, combine taco seasoning mix with soy crumbles. Evenly distribute seasoned crumbles over the tomatoes with chilies. Sprinkle both cheeses over the "meat" layer.

Bake in the oven for about 13 minutes, until tortilla edges have browned and cheese has melted. Plate it up, top with sour cream, and dig in!

MAKES 1 SERVING

 For a pic of this recipe, see the second photo insert. Yay!

HG Tip! Ro*tel Original Diced Tomatoes & Green Chilies is THE BEST product to use for this recipe. Find it!

blt salad wrap

PER SERVING (entire recipe): 185 calories, 5.5g fat, 983mg sodium, 23.5g carbs, 13g fiber, 4g sugars, 20.5g protein

If you dig the famous Hacked 'n Whacked BLT Salad from our first book, you'll enjoy chomping into this wrap.

Ingredients

1 large La Tortilla Factory Smart & Delicious Low Carb/High Fiber tortilla
4 slices extra-lean turkey bacon
1 plum tomato (preferably Roma), chopped
½ cup shredded lettuce
1 tablespoon fat-free mayonnaise

Directions

Cook bacon according to package directions, either in the microwave or in a pan sprayed with nonstick spray. Once cool enough to handle, roughly chop.

Microwave tortilla until slightly warm. Lay tortilla flat and spread mayo over it, leaving about 1 inch of space around the perimeter.

Place lettuce in the center of the tortilla. Top with chopped bacon and tomato.

Wrap tortilla up by folding in the sides first, and then rolling it up tightly from the bottom. Enjoy!

MAKES 1 SERVING

Chew on This

In the 1920s, the word "tomato" was slang for a good-looking woman. The Aztecs called tomatoes "*xitomatl*," which means "plump thing with a navel." Hmmm, forget "tomato." How about you just say we're pretty . . . ?

extreme mega-supreme pizza pocket

PER SERVING (entire recipe): 196 calories, 6g fat, 1,215mg sodium, 26.5g carbs, 13g fiber, 4.5g sugars, 19g protein

How many guilt-free pizza-like items can be crammed into one book? MANY!!! (But never TOO many.)

Ingredients

1 large La Tortilla Factory Smart & Delicious Low Carb/High Fiber tortilla
1 wedge The Laughing Cow Light Original Swiss cheese
3 tablespoons shredded fat-free mozzarella cheese
¼ cup canned tomato sauce with Italian seasonings
4 slices turkey pepperoni, chopped
2 tablespoons chopped green bell pepper
2 tablespoons chopped onion
2 tablespoons chopped mushrooms

Directions

Preheat oven to 350 degrees.

Warm tortilla in the microwave for 10 seconds. Lay tortilla flat and spread cheese wedge down the center.

In a medium bowl, combine all of the veggies with the tomato sauce until well mixed. Place this mixture on top of the spread cheese wedge in the center of the tortilla.

Sprinkle pepperoni on top of the veggie mixture. Top with the shredded cheese.

Wrap tortilla up by folding in the sides first, and then rolling it up tightly from the bottom.

Spray a baking sheet lightly with nonstick spray. Place your wrap on the sheet, seam side down. Bake in the oven for 10 to 15 minutes, or until tortilla is slightly browned.

MAKES 1 SERVING

cheeseburger quesadilla

PER SERVING (entire quesadilla): 186 calories, 3.5g fat, 989mg sodium, 27g carbs, 16g fiber, 2.5g sugars, 26g protein

Part burger. Part Mexican tortilla treat. Anything and EVERYTHING can be turned into a quesadilla these days. This recipe is proof.

Ingredients

1 large La Tortilla Factory Smart & Delicious Low Carb/High Fiber tortilla
1 Boca Original Meatless Burger, thawed
1 slice fat-free American cheese, chopped
1 tablespoon chopped onion
1 tablespoon chopped pickles
Optional ingredients: salt, black pepper, garlic powder
Optional topping: ketchup

Directions

Preheat oven to 350 degrees.

Cut burger into small bite-sized pieces. Bring a pan sprayed with nonstick spray to medium heat on the stove. Add onion and burger pieces. Cook for 2 to 3 minutes, until onion is soft. Season mixture to taste with optional ingredients, if you like.

Spray a medium-large baking sheet lightly with nonstick spray. Lay tortilla flat on the sheet and evenly top with the cheese pieces. Bake in the oven for about 2 minutes, until cheese has melted slightly. Leave oven on.

Spread burger mixture over one half of the tortilla. Top with pickles and fold tortilla in half, pressing down lightly with a spatula to seal.

Bake in the oven for another 3 to 5 minutes, until tortilla edges are slightly brown.

Remove from the oven and cut into triangles. Top or serve with ketchup, if you like. Yum!

MAKES 1 SERVING

For a pic of this recipe, see the second photo insert. Yay!

Chew on This

Denny's Beer Barrel Pub in Clearfield, Pennsylvania, is touted as having "possibly the world's largest hamburgers." The menu features the 15-pound Belly Buster, the Belly Bruiser (50+ pounds), and the Main Event Burger (a.k.a. the Charity Burger)—that thing weighs in at more than 100 pounds. Yikes!

little taco salad in a shell

PER SERVING (entire recipe): 178 calories, 4.25g fat, 919mg sodium, 28g carbs, 15.5g fiber, 4g sugars, 21g protein

This taco salad is soooooo adorable. It's like a mini version of one you'd get at a restaurant . . . complete with a crunchy taco shell and all the delicious toppings!

◌ Ingredients

1 large La Tortilla Factory Smart & Delicious Low Carb/High Fiber tortilla

1½ cups shredded lettuce

⅓ cup frozen ground-beef-style soy crumbles

2 tablespoons shredded fat-free cheddar cheese

½ teaspoon dry taco seasoning mix

2 tablespoons salsa

1 tablespoon fat-free sour cream

◌ Directions

Preheat oven to 425 degrees.

Spray a small round casserole dish (about 6 inches in diameter) with nonstick spray. Gently push tortilla into the dish, so that the sides of the tortilla fold in and rest along the sides of the dish. The tortilla should take on a bowl or "shell" shape.

Bake tortilla bowl in the oven for 10 to 12 minutes, until crispy. Set aside until cool.

Place soy crumbles in small microwave-safe dish and cover with taco seasoning mix. Microwave for 30 seconds, then stir well. Microwave for an additional 10 to 20 seconds, until hot.

Fill the tortilla "shell" with lettuce and top with seasoned soy crumbles. Sprinkle cheese on top. Finish with salsa and sour cream. Dig in!

MAKES 1 SERVING

 For a pic of this recipe, see the second photo insert. Yay!

For Weight Watchers **POINTS**®
values and photos of all the
recipes in this book, check out
hungry-girl.com/book.

chapter eight

shivering sips

Smoothies, Slushies, and Shakes

A blender is a beautiful thing, people. Toss a few key ingredients in, turn it on, and voilà—you've got a fantastic low-calorie beverage. Okay, it's not *that* simple. Great recipes help. No worries—HG's got you covered. Smoothies, shakes, slushies, Swappuccinos . . . they're all here. So get busy, Blendy!

joe cool java freeze

PER SERVING (entire drink): 68 calories, 3.75g fat, 55mg sodium, 6.5g carbs, <0.5g fiber, 1g sugars, 1.5g protein

This is 50 percent iced coffee, 50 percent slushie dessert.
And 100 percent DELICIOUS!!!

Ingredients

¼ cup light vanilla soymilk, cold

4 teaspoons Coffee-mate Sugar Free French Vanilla powdered creamer

1 teaspoon instant coffee granules

2 no-calorie sweetener packets

1½ cups crushed ice *or* 8 to 10 ice cubes

Directions

In a tall glass, combine powdered creamer, coffee granules, and sweetener with ¼ cup hot water. Stir until ingredients have dissolved. Add ½ cup cold water and stir.

Transfer coffee mixture to a blender with soymilk and ice. Mix at low to medium speed until shake is just blended, but not liquefied. Pour into your glass and slurp it up!

MAKES 1 SERVING

For Weight Watchers *POINTS*® values and photos of all the recipes in this book, check out hungry-girl.com/book.

cravin' cap'n crunch shake

PER SERVING (entire shake): 192 calories, 2.75g fat, 219mg sodium, 35g carbs, 2.5g fiber, 17g sugars, 7g protein

Who else would DARE put a shake made with sugary breakfast cereal in a guilt-free cookbook? No one!!!

Ingredients

⅔ cup light vanilla soymilk, cold
½ cup fat-free vanilla ice cream
¼ cup Cap'n Crunch cereal (original)
2 tablespoons sugar-free calorie-free vanilla syrup
1 teaspoon Coffee-mate Sugar Free French Vanilla powdered creamer
¼ teaspoon vanilla extract
2 no-calorie sweetener packets
¾ cup crushed ice *or* 4 to 6 ice cubes
Optional topping: Fat Free Reddi-wip

Directions

In a small bowl or glass, dissolve powdered creamer in 1 tablespoon warm water. Transfer to a blender.

Add all of the other ingredients to the blender and blend until your ideal consistency is reached.

Pour your shake into a glass. Top it off with some Reddi-wip, if you like.

MAKES 1 SERVING

 For a pic of this recipe, see the second photo insert. Yay!

HG Fast Fact:

Thanks for the good idea, Carl's Jr.! You and your crazy-fatty, turbo-sugared-up mess of a milkshake inspired our dream drink made of cereal and ice cream. Only ours has less than one-tenth the fat and 500 fewer calories. *And*, um, it's still around!

frozen fudge chip freeze

PER SERVING (entire drink): 138 calories, 4.5g fat, 184mg sodium, 22g carbs, 1.5g fiber, 13g sugars, 4g protein

The chocolate chips add TONS of flavor to this coffee shop swap!

Ingredients

One 25-calorie packet diet hot cocoa mix
¼ cup light vanilla soymilk, cold
1 tablespoon sugar-free chocolate syrup
1 tablespoon mini semi-sweet chocolate chips
2 no-calorie sweetener packets
1 cup crushed ice *or* 5 to 8 ice cubes
2 tablespoons Fat Free Reddi-wip

Directions

In a tall glass, combine cocoa mix with ½ cup warm water. Stir until cocoa mix has dissolved, then transfer to a blender.

Add soymilk, chocolate syrup, chocolate chips, sweetener, and ice to the blender. Blend on high speed for 30 to 45 seconds.

Pour into your glass and top with Reddi-wip. Slurp!

MAKES 1 SERVING

raspberry mocha
madness swappuccino

PER SERVING (entire drink): 82 calories, 1.75g fat, 80mg sodium,
15.5g carbs, 1g fiber, 8g sugars, 3g protein

This frozen treat is REALLY delicious. Try to find Torani Sugar Free Syrup
because it is far and away the BEST kind out there.

▭ Ingredients

½ cup light chocolate soymilk, cold
¼ cup sugar-free calorie-free raspberry syrup
1½ teaspoons instant coffee granules
1 teaspoon Coffee-mate Sugar Free French Vanilla powdered creamer
1 teaspoon unsweetened cocoa
2 no-calorie sweetener packets
1½ cups crushed ice *or* 8 to 10 ice cubes
2 tablespoons Fat Free Reddi-wip

▭ Directions

In a tall glass, combine coffee granules, powdered creamer, cocoa, and sweetener. Add 2 tablespoons hot water and stir to dissolve ingredients.

Add soymilk and raspberry syrup, then transfer to a blender. Add ice and blend on high speed until thoroughly mixed.

Pour into your glass and finish off with whipped topping. Enjoy!

MAKES 1 SERVING

 For a pic of this recipe, see the second photo insert. Yay!

pb & j super-shake

PER SERVING (entire shake): 199 calories, 7.25g fat,
291mg sodium, 29.5g carbs, 3g fiber, 12g sugars, 6g protein

Here's a way to enjoy peanut butter and jelly without all of the fat and calories.

Ingredients

⅔ cup Unsweetened Original Almond Breeze, cold
⅓ cup fat-free vanilla ice cream
¼ cup Reese's Puffs cereal (original)
2 frozen unsweetened strawberries, partially thawed
2 teaspoons reduced-fat peanut butter
1 no-calorie sweetener packet
⅔ cup crushed ice *or* 3 to 5 ice cubes
Optional topping: Fat Free Reddi-wip

Directions

Place all ingredients except for the optional Reddi-wip in a blender. Blend at high speed until thoroughly mixed.

Pour the shake into a glass and, if you like, top it off with Reddi-wip. PB-rific!

MAKES 1 SERVING

HG Alternative!

If you can't get your hands on the Almond Breeze, you can use plain light soymilk instead—your shake will clock in with about 213 calories (STILL WORTH IT!).

chocolate chip cookie crisp puddin' shake

PER SERVING (entire shake): 198 calories, 3.75g fat, 321mg sodium, 37g carbs, 1g fiber, 16.5g sugars, 5g protein

Yup, it's another recipe that calls for sugary breakfast cereal. Used with extreme caution, of course!

Ingredients

1 Jell-O Sugar Free Vanilla Pudding Snack
⅔ cup light chocolate soymilk, cold
⅓ cup Cookie Crisp cereal (original)
1 teaspoon mini semi-sweet chocolate chips
1 no-calorie sweetener packet
¾ cup crushed ice or 4 to 6 ice cubes
Optional toppings: Fat Free Reddi-wip,
    additional mini semi-sweet chocolate chips

Directions

Place all ingredients except for the optional toppings in a blender. Blend at high speed until thoroughly mixed.

Pour the shake into a glass and, if you like, top it off with the Reddi-wip and a few extra mini chocolate chips. Cookie-licious!

MAKES 1 SERVING

green tea crème swappuccino

PER SERVING (entire drink): 75 calories, 2.5g fat, 96mg sodium, 8g carbs, 1g fiber, 4g sugars, 3g protein

This creamy treat infused with green tea is FANTASTIC. Many think it's better than the Starbucks version. Try it for yourself and see.

Ingredients

½ cup light vanilla soymilk, cold
2 tablespoons sugar-free calorie-free vanilla syrup
2 teaspoons Coffee-mate Sugar Free French Vanilla powdered creamer
1 heaping teaspoon matcha green tea powder
2 no-calorie sweetener packets
1½ cups crushed ice *or* 8 to 10 ice cubes
2 tablespoons Fat Free Reddi-wip

HG Heads Up!
You can find matcha green tea powder in tea shops, at select markets, and online.

Directions

In a tall glass, combine green tea powder and powdered creamer with ¼ cup warm water. Stir until powders have completely dissolved.

Transfer green tea mixture to a blender. Add soymilk, syrup, sweetener, and ice. Blend on high speed for about 30 seconds.

Pour into your glass and top with Reddi-wip. Yum!

MAKES 1 SERVING

For Weight Watchers *POINTS*® values and photos of all the recipes in this book, check out hungry-girl.com/book.

mint chocolate chip freeze

PER SERVING (entire drink): 87 calories, 4.75g fat, 36mg sodium, 12g carbs, 0g fiber, 3g sugars, <0.5g protein

You'll like this chilly sip even if you don't like mint. And if you are a mint fan, you'll REALLY dig it!

Ingredients

1 tablespoon Coffee-mate Sugar Free French Vanilla powdered creamer

1 tablespoon sugar-free chocolate syrup

1 teaspoon instant coffee granules

1 teaspoon mini semi-sweet chocolate chips

¼ teaspoon spearmint or peppermint extract

2 no-calorie sweetener packets

1 cup crushed ice *or* 5 to 8 ice cubes

2 tablespoons Chocolate Reddi-wip

Directions

In a tall glass, combine powdered creamer with 2 tablespoons warm water. Stir until powder has dissolved. Add ¾ cup cold water and transfer mixture to a blender.

Add all of the other ingredients except for the Reddi-wip to the blender. Blend on high speed for 30 to 45 seconds.

Pour into your glass and top with Chocolate Reddi-wip. Enjoy!

MAKES 1 SERVING

freckled lemonade

Lemonade . . . with freckles? YES!!! Thanks to our lovely friend the strawberry, your lemon slush will, in fact, be all speckled. Cute!

This recipe was co-developed with Weight Watchers®.

Ingredients

One-half 2-serving packet (about ½ teaspoon) sugar-free lemonade powdered drink mix
1 cup diet lemon-lime soda, cold
4 frozen unsweetened strawberries
1 no-calorie sweetener packet
⅔ cup crushed ice *or* 3 to 5 ice cubes

Directions

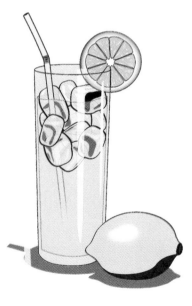

In a tall glass, combine drink mix, soda, and sweetener with ¼ to ½ cup cold water (depending on how sweet you like your lemonade). Stir until drink mix has dissolved.

Pour the lemonade mixture into a blender. Add frozen strawberries and ice to the blender. Blend until smooth.

Pour into your glass and sip away!

MAKES 1 SERVING

too-good two-berry citrus smoothie

PER SERVING (entire smoothie): 101 calories, 0.5g fat, 4mg sodium, 24g carbs, 5g fiber, 13g sugars, 1g protein

Two berries. Too good. The title says it all.

Ingredients

1 cup frozen unsweetened strawberries
½ cup frozen unsweetened blueberries
One-half 2-serving packet (about ½ teaspoon) sugar-free orange powdered drink mix
1 no-calorie sweetener packet

Directions

Place frozen berries in a blender and allow to thaw slightly, 1 to 2 minutes.

Meanwhile, in a tall glass, combine powdered drink mix and sweetener with 1¼ cups cold water. Stir well, then transfer to the blender.

Blend smoothie mixture at medium-high speed until thoroughly mixed. If blending slows, stop blender, stir mixture, and blend again. Pour into your glass and drink up!

MAKES 1 SERVING

chocolate-banana smoothie

PER SERVING (entire smoothie): 164 calories, 1.5g fat, 137mg sodium, 35.5g carbs, 3.75g fiber, 18g sugars, 3g protein

Chocolate and banana are ALWAYS great together. Don't miss our Funky Monkey Squares on page 246.

Ingredients

One 25-calorie packet diet hot cocoa mix
1 small ripe banana, sliced and frozen
2 teaspoons fat-free non-dairy powdered creamer
1 teaspoon mini semi-sweet chocolate chips
1 no-calorie sweetener packet
1 cup crushed ice *or* 5 to 8 ice cubes

Directions

In a tall glass, combine cocoa mix, powdered creamer, chocolate chips, and sweetener. Add ¼ cup very hot water and stir until ingredients have dissolved. Add ½ cup cold water and stir.

Transfer contents of the glass to a blender. Add frozen banana slices and ice. Blend at medium speed until completely mixed. Pour into your glass and enjoy!

MAKES 1 SERVING

freezy-cool lemon slushie

PER SERVING (entire slushie): 30 calories, 0g fat, 140mg sodium, 2g carbs, 0g fiber, 0g sugars, 0g protein

This stuff is as good as any frozen lemonade or sweet lemon slushie you'd find ANYWHERE. And it's insanely low in calories. The non-dairy creamer (our little secret) adds the PERFECT amount of richness to this tangy treat.

Ingredients

Two 2-serving packets sugar-free lemonade powdered drink mix
1 teaspoon fat-free non-dairy powdered creamer
1½ cups crushed ice *or* 8 to 10 ice cubes

Directions

In a tall glass, combine powdered creamer with ¼ cup warm water. Stir until creamer has dissolved.

Add 1¼ cups cold water and powdered drink mix, and mix thoroughly.

Transfer contents of the glass to a blender and add ice. Blend at high speed until thoroughly blended.

Pour into your glass and spoon or sip your way to lemony satisfaction!

MAKES 1 SERVING

HG Tip! If you like your slushie practically frozen, place in the freezer for about 20 minutes before you slurp it.

mango-tango slushie

PER SERVING (entire slushie): 40 calories, 0g fat, 43mg sodium, 10g carbs, 1g fiber, 7.5g sugars, 0g protein

Frozen and tropical, this recipe is a great way to cool down by the pool. Or drink it indoors and pretend you're by a pool . . .

Ingredients

¾ cup Diet V8 Splash Tropical Blend, cold
¼ cup frozen unsweetened mango chunks
¼ of a 2-serving packet (about ¼ teaspoon) sugar-free lemonade powdered drink mix
1 cup crushed ice *or* 5 to 8 ice cubes

Directions

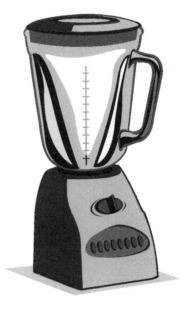

Place all ingredients in a blender and blend until smooth. Drink up!

MAKES 1 SERVING

key lime pie shake

PER SERVING (entire shake): 124 calories, 1.25g fat,
122mg sodium, 24g carbs, 1.5g fiber, 13g sugars, 4.5g protein

*So creamy, so tart, so delicious! Spike it with lime vodka
and turn it into a dessert martini. Yum!*

Ingredients

½ cup light vanilla soymilk, cold
¼ cup fat-free vanilla ice cream
2 tablespoons canned crushed pineapple in juice
2 tablespoons sugar-free calorie-free vanilla syrup
1 tablespoon lime juice
1 no-calorie sweetener packet
¾ cup crushed ice *or* 4 to 6 ice cubes
2 tablespoons Fat Free Reddi-wip
¼ sheet (1 cracker) low-fat honey graham
    crackers, crushed

Directions

Combine soymilk, ice cream, pineapple, vanilla
syrup, lime juice, sweetener, and ice in a blender. Blend on high speed for 30 to 45 seconds.

Pour shake into a glass and top with Reddi-wip. Finish it off with the crushed graham cracker.

MAKES 1 SERVING

For a pic of this recipe, see the second photo insert. Yay!

HG Fast Fact:

Key lime pie is the state pie of Florida. But our
recipe can be enjoyed by humans in every state.

piña colada smoothie

Pineapple and coconut live together here in one tall glass of deliciousness. Woohoo!

Ingredients

¼ cup fat-free vanilla ice cream
¼ cup pineapple juice, cold
3 tablespoons sugar-free calorie-free coconut syrup
1 tablespoon canned crushed pineapple in juice
1 cup crushed ice *or* 5 to 8 ice cubes

Directions

Place all ingredients in a blender. Blend on high speed for about 30 seconds, until mixture is smooth and completely blended. Pour and enjoy!

MAKES 1 SERVING

HG Alternative!

No coconut syrup? No problem! In its place, just add 3 tablespoons water, ¾ teaspoon coconut extract, and 2¼ teaspoons Splenda No Calorie Sweetener (granulated). Crisis averted.

no-name peachy pumpkin drink

PER SERVING (entire drink): 118 calories, 1g fat, 82mg sodium, 20g carbs, 3.75g fiber, 11g sugars, 6g protein

Not sure why this doesn't have a name because it's a totally unique, fruity, blended tea drink—and it's GREAT! If you like pumpkin, it'll end up becoming one of your early morning staples.

Ingredients

½ cup Snapple Diet Peach Iced Tea, cold
½ cup canned pure pumpkin
¼ cup light vanilla soymilk, cold
3 ounces fat-free vanilla yogurt
2 no-calorie sweetener packets
¼ teaspoon pumpkin pie spice
1 cup crushed ice *or* 5 to 8 ice cubes
Optional: 1 to 2 tablespoons sugar-free calorie-free peach syrup

HG Heads Up!
If you can get your hands on Torani Sugar Free Peach Syrup, DO IT! It makes this recipe even better.

Directions

Place all ingredients in a blender and blend on high for 30 to 45 seconds.

Add a tablespoon or two of the SF peach syrup, if you like. Enjoy!!!!

MAKES 1 SERVING

For Weight Watchers *POINTS*® values and photos of all the recipes in this book, check out hungry-girl.com/book.

Cakes! In Cups! With Frosting (Sometimes)!

Who would have guessed that an entire chapter devoted to CUPCAKES could exist in a guilt-free cookbook? Bold, creative, brilliant, innovative thinkers who can predict the future, that's who. And here you have it. A whole chapter dedicated to cupcakes—right here in this completely guilt-free cookbook. And yes, each cupcake clocks in with less than 200 calories. In fact, each one has less than 150! Ready to go cupcake crazy? Good!

crazy-crumbly super-yummy coffee cakes

PER SERVING (1 cupcake with crumb topping): 118 calories, 2g fat, 196mg sodium, 24g carbs, 2.5g fiber, 11g sugars, 2.5g protein

These mini coffee cakes are melt-in-your-mouth good. They have that sweet crumbly topping and everything!

Ingredients

Heads Up, F1 Fans! Don't miss our Fun with Fiber One chapter, starting on page 282.

For Cupcakes
2 cups moist-style yellow cake mix (½ of an 18.25-ounce box)

¾ cup fat-free sour cream

¼ cup fat-free liquid egg substitute

¼ cup sugar-free calorie-free hazelnut syrup

1 teaspoon cinnamon

For Crumb Topping
1 cup Fiber One bran cereal (original)

2 tablespoons plus 2 teaspoons
   fat-free liquid egg substitute

2 tablespoons plus 2 teaspoons
   no-sugar-added applesauce

2 tablespoons Splenda No Calorie
   Sweetener (granulated)

2 teaspoons brown sugar (not packed)

2 teaspoons cinnamon

Directions

Preheat oven to 350 degrees.

To make the crumb topping, grind Fiber One in a food processor or blender to a breadcrumb-like consistency. Transfer crumbs to a medium mixing bowl and add all of the other topping ingredients. Stir with a fork until completely mixed. Then use the fork to break mixture up into small crumbles. Set aside.

In a large mixing bowl, combine all of the cupcake ingredients. Stir until thoroughly blended and free of lumps.

Line a 12-cup muffin pan with baking cups and/or spray with nonstick spray. Evenly distribute cake mixture among the cups. Evenly top each cupcake with crumb mixture, using your fingers to help form the crumbs.

Bake in the oven for about 15 minutes, until a toothpick inserted into the center of a cupcake comes out clean. Allow cupcakes to cool before removing cakes from the pan. Yummmm!

MAKES 12 SERVINGS

For a pic of this recipe, see the second photo insert. Yay!

For Weight Watchers *POINTS*® values and photos of all the recipes in this book, check out hungry-girl.com/book.

red velvet insanity cupcakes

PER SERVING (1 frosted cupcake): 140 calories, 3g fat, 262mg sodium, 24.5g carbs, 0.5g fiber, 15g sugars, 3g protein

You'd have to be insane to not flip over these brightly colored little cakes.

Ingredients

For Cupcakes

1 cup moist-style devil's food cake mix (¼ of an 18.25-ounce box)

1 cup moist-style yellow cake mix (¼ of an 18.25-ounce box)

Two 25-calorie packets diet hot cocoa mix

½ cup fat-free liquid egg substitute

¼ cup mini semi-sweet chocolate chips, divided

1 tablespoon red food coloring

1 teaspoon Splenda No Calorie Sweetener (granulated)

⅛ teaspoon salt

For Frosting

6 tablespoons Jet-Puffed Marshmallow Creme

6 tablespoons Cool Whip Free, thawed

¼ cup fat-free cream cheese, room temperature

1 tablespoon Splenda No Calorie Sweetener (granulated)

Directions

Preheat oven to 350 degrees.

In a medium mixing bowl, combine all frosting ingredients except for the Cool Whip until mixed well. Fold in Cool Whip and refrigerate until cupcakes are ready to be frosted.

In a tall glass, place half of the mini chocolate chips and the contents of both cocoa packets. Add ½ cup boiling water and stir until chips and cocoa mix have dissolved.

Add 1 cup cold water and mix well.

Pour cocoa mixture into a large mixing bowl. Add cake mixes, egg substitute, remaining chocolate chips, food coloring, Splenda, and salt. Whisk for about 2 minutes, until smooth and blended. Batter will be thin, but don't worry—your cupcakes will puff up once baked!

Line a 12-cup muffin pan with baking cups and/or spray with nonstick spray. Evenly distribute batter among the cups. Bake in the oven for 15 to 20 minutes. Cupcakes will look shiny when done.

Allow cupcakes to cool completely, then evenly distribute the frosting over the tops. Enjoy!

MAKES 12 SERVINGS

📷 **For a pic of this recipe, see the second photo insert. Yay!**

14-carat cupcakes

Lots of people think carrot cake is low in calories because it's made with carrots. No chance. In fact, carrot cake often has MORE calories and fat than white or chocolate cake. Our guilt-free version, however, is low in calories and fat. It also rocks!!!

Ingredients

For Cupcakes
1½ cups shredded carrots, roughly chopped if shreds are long
1 cup moist-style yellow cake mix (¼ of an 18.25-ounce box)
¾ cup whole-wheat flour
¾ cup canned pure pumpkin
⅔ cup fat-free liquid egg substitute
⅔ cup canned crushed pineapple in juice (not drained)
½ cup Splenda No Calorie Sweetener (granulated)
¼ cup raisins (not packed)
2 tablespoons brown sugar (not packed)
1½ teaspoons pumpkin pie spice
1½ teaspoons cinnamon
1 teaspoon baking powder

For Frosting
4 ounces fat-free cream cheese, room temperature
⅓ cup plain fat-free Greek yogurt
⅔ cup Splenda No Calorie Sweetener (granulated)
½ teaspoon vanilla extract

Directions

Preheat oven to 350 degrees.

In a medium mixing bowl, combine all frosting ingredients. Using a whisk or fork, blend until smooth. Refrigerate until cupcakes are ready to be frosted.

In a large mixing bowl, combine cake mix, flour, Splenda, brown sugar, pumpkin pie spice, cinnamon, and baking powder. Mix well and set aside.

In a medium mixing bowl, combine pumpkin and egg substitute with ¼ cup water, stirring until blended.

Add pumpkin mixture to the large bowl. Using a whisk or fork, blend contents of the large bowl until just mixed. Stir in carrots, pineapple, and raisins.

Line a 12-cup muffin pan with baking cups and/or spray with nonstick spray. Evenly distribute cake mixture among the cups.

Bake in the oven for 20 to 25 minutes, until a toothpick inserted into the center of a cupcake comes out clean.

Allow cupcakes to cool completely, then evenly distribute frosting over the tops. Refrigerate until frosting has set and you're ready to serve.

MAKES 12 SERVINGS

Chew on This

A slice of carrot cake from Denny's has (are you sitting down?) 820 calories and 45 grams fat! Please don't blame those poor, defenseless carrots. They have nothing to do with it!

chocolate marshmallow madness cupcakes

PER SERVING (1 glazed and topped cupcake): 109 calories, 2g fat, 230mg sodium, 21g carbs, 0.75g fiber, 12.5g sugars, 2g protein

Chocolatey, gooey marshmallow goodness in cute little cupcake form. Love. It.

Ingredients

HG Heads Up! These are best the day they are prepared.

For Cupcakes
2 cups moist-style chocolate cake mix (½ of an 18.25-ounce box)
One 25-calorie packet diet hot cocoa mix
½ cup fat-free liquid egg substitute
1 tablespoon Splenda No Calorie Sweetener (granulated)
⅛ teaspoon salt

For Glaze
¼ cup Jet-Puffed Marshmallow Creme
1 teaspoon light vanilla soymilk

For Topping
1 tablespoon mini semi-sweet chocolate chips
12 mini marshmallows

Directions

Preheat oven to 350 degrees.

In a tall glass, combine cocoa mix with ¼ cup hot water. Stir until cocoa dissolves. Add 1 cup cold water and stir well.

In a large mixing bowl, combine cake mix, Splenda, and salt. Add egg substitute and cocoa mixture, then whisk until smooth.

Line a 12-cup muffin pan with baking cups and/or spray with nonstick spray. Evenly distribute cake mixture among the cups.

Bake in the oven for about 15 minutes, until a toothpick inserted into the center of a cupcake comes out clean. Remove from oven and let cool.

To prepare glaze, place marshmallow creme in a small dish. Add soymilk and mix well.

Once cupcakes have cooled completely, drizzle marshmallow glaze over them. Top each cupcake with ¼ teaspoon chocolate chips and one mini marshmallow. Refrigerate until ready to serve.

MAKES 12 SERVINGS

For a pic of this recipe, see the second photo insert. Yay!

For Weight Watchers *POINTS*® values and photos of all the recipes in this book, check out hungry-girl.com/book.

iced 'n spiced
pumpkin puddin' cupcakes

PER SERVING (1 frosted cupcake): 112 calories, 1.75g fat,
200mg sodium, 22g carbs, 0.5g fiber, 12g sugars, 2g protein

Yeah, we know these are really more "frosted" than "iced," but Frosted 'n Spiced Pumpkin Puddin' Cupcakes just doesn't have the same ring to it...

Ingredients

For Cupcakes
2 cups moist-style spice cake mix (½ of an 18.25-ounce box)
1 cup canned pure pumpkin
⅓ cup fat-free liquid egg substitute
⅛ teaspoon salt

For Frosting
½ cup plus 1 tablespoon Cool Whip Free, thawed
2 tablespoons Splenda No Calorie
    Sweetener (granulated)
2 tablespoons fat-free cream cheese,
    room temperature
1 tablespoon canned pure pumpkin
1 teaspoon sugar-free fat-free vanilla
    instant pudding mix
⅛ teaspoon cinnamon

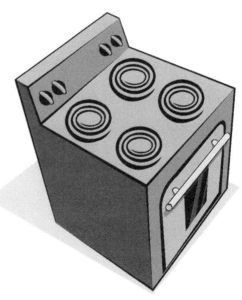

Directions

Preheat oven to 350 degrees.

In a medium mixing bowl, combine all of
the frosting ingredients, stirring until well
mixed. Refrigerate until cupcakes are
ready to be frosted.

In a large mixing bowl, combine all of the cupcake ingredients with ½ cup water. Mix until blended.

Line a 12-cup muffin pan with baking cups and/or spray with nonstick spray. Evenly distribute cake mixture among the cups.

Bake in the oven for about 15 minutes, until a toothpick inserted into the center of a cupcake comes out clean.

Cool cupcakes completely, and evenly distribute frosting among the tops. Yum!

MAKES 12 SERVINGS

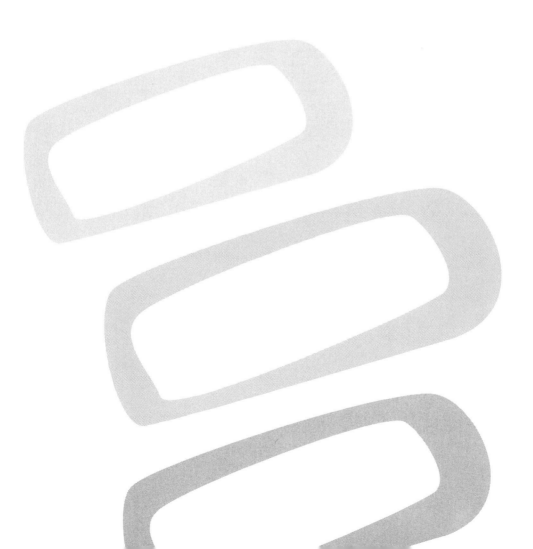

razzle dazzle chocolate raspberry cupcakes

PER SERVING (1 frosted cupcake): 124 calories, 2g fat, 259mg sodium, 23.5g carbs, 2g fiber, 12.5g sugars, 2g protein

Raspberry and chocolate have been hanging out together FOREVER. But now things are getting serious ... These cakes are decadent and frosted yet STILL have just 124 calories each!

Ingredients

For Cupcakes
2 cups moist-style chocolate cake mix (½ of an 18.25-ounce box)
Two 25-calorie packets diet hot cocoa mix
1½ cups raspberries
¼ cup fat-free liquid egg substitute
1 tablespoon mini semi-sweet chocolate chips
1 no-calorie sweetener packet
¼ teaspoon baking powder
⅛ teaspoon salt

For Frosting
1 Jell-O Sugar Free Double Chocolate Pudding Snack
2 tablespoons chocolate frosting

Optional Topping
12 additional raspberries

Directions

Preheat oven to 350 degrees.

To make frosting, place pudding in a small dish. Add chocolate frosting and stir until mixed thoroughly. Refrigerate until cupcakes are ready to be frosted.

HG Fast Fact:

Ounce for ounce, fresh raspberries have more fiber than even broccoli. Shocking yet exciting!

Place contents of cocoa and sweetener packets in a tall glass. Add chocolate chips. Cover with ½ cup boiling water and stir until ingredients have dissolved. Add ¼ cup cold water and stir again.

Transfer cocoa mixture to a blender. Add raspberries and egg substitute. Puree until blended.

In a large mixing bowl, combine cake mix, baking powder, and salt. Add pureed cocoa mixture to the bowl and stir until completely blended, about 2 minutes.

Line a 12-cup muffin pan with baking cups and/or spray with nonstick spray. Evenly distribute cake mixture among the cups.

Bake in the oven for about 15 minutes, until a toothpick inserted into the center of a cupcake comes out clean.

Allow cupcakes to cool completely, then evenly distribute frosting among the tops. Finish each off with a raspberry, if you like. Refrigerate until ready to serve.

MAKES 12 SERVINGS

HG Alternative!

Feel like saving time and calories? Skip the frosting. Each frosting-free cupcake has 108 calories, 2 grams fat, 20 grams carbs, and 2 grams fiber.

death by chocolate cone cakes

PER SERVING (1 Cone Cake with toppings): 93 calories, 2.5g fat, 130mg sodium, 16g carbs, 0.5g fiber, 8g sugars, 1g protein

These are the cutest little cake treats EVER. And they're perfect at parties—for kids and adults!

Ingredients

HG Heads Up!
These are best the day they are prepared.

For Cone Cakes
12 cake (flat-bottom) cones
1 cup moist-style chocolate cake mix (¼ of an 18.25-ounce box)
One 25-calorie packet diet hot cocoa mix
¼ cup fat-free liquid egg substitute
2 teaspoons mini semi-sweet chocolate chips

For Topping
1 Jell-O Sugar Free Double Chocolate Pudding Snack
2 tablespoons chocolate frosting
2 tablespoons rainbow sprinkles

Directions

Preheat oven to 350 degrees.

In a medium mixing bowl, combine pudding and frosting, stirring until mixed well. Refrigerate until Cone Cakes are ready to be frosted.

Place mini chocolate chips and the contents of cocoa packet in a tall glass. Add ¼ cup boiling water. Stir until chips and cocoa mix have dissolved. Add ¼ cup cold water and stir well.

Place cake mix in a large mixing bowl. Add cocoa mixture and egg substitute, and whip batter with a whisk or fork for 2 minutes. Set aside.

Find an area near the oven to assemble Cone Cakes, so that you do not have to move them very far. Check the bottom of the cones for uneven ridges, removing any so that cones sit flat. Place each cone upright in a cup of a 12-cup muffin pan.

Carefully spoon batter into cones until cones are a little more than halfway full. Allow cones to sit for a few minutes while batter settles.

VERY carefully transfer pan to the oven. Bake for 15 to 20 minutes, until a toothpick inserted into the center comes out clean.

Cool Cone Cakes completely, then evenly distribute frosting mixture over the cupcakes, covering the tops entirely.

Add ½ teaspoon sprinkles to the top of each frosted Cone Cake. Try not to pass out when you see how adorable these are and how good they taste!

MAKES 12 SERVINGS

 For a pic of this recipe, see the second photo insert. Yay!

HG Tip! These things are top-heavy once they're frosted, so DO NOT try to balance 'em on a tray with one hand!

piña colada cupcakes

PER SERVING (1 frosted cupcake): 115 calories, 1.75g fat,
171mg sodium, 23g carbs, <0.5g fiber, 13.5g sugars, 1g protein

These pineapple coconut cupcakes are a sweet, tropical
cupcake dream come true. Weeeeeee!

Ingredients

For Cupcakes

2 cups moist-style yellow cake mix (½ of an 18.25-ounce box)

1½ eight-ounce cans crushed pineapple in juice (not drained)

½ teaspoon coconut extract

For Frosting

4 ounces canned crushed pineapple in juice (drained)

1 Jell-O Sugar Free Vanilla Pudding Snack

1½ tablespoons fat-free cream cheese,
   room temperature

⅛ teaspoon coconut extract

1 no-calorie sweetener packet

Directions

Preheat oven to 350 degrees.

In a medium mixing bowl, combine
all frosting ingredients and mix until
blended. Refrigerate until cupcakes
are ready to be frosted.

In a large mixing bowl, combine cake mix with undrained pineapple. Add coconut extract and mix until thoroughly blended.

Line a 12-cup muffin pan with baking cups and/or spray with nonstick spray. Evenly distribute cake mixture among the cups.

Bake in the oven for about 20 minutes, until a toothpick inserted into the center of a cupcake comes out clean.

Allow cupcakes to cool completely, then evenly distribute frosting over the tops. Refrigerate until ready to serve. Time for a cake-tastic, tropical fiesta!

MAKES 12 SERVINGS

Chew on This

An average 8-ounce piña colada packs in about 350 calories and over 10 grams fat. Quadruple that if you down one of the ginormous restaurant versions. Have one of these cupcakes instead.

strawberry shortycakes

These cupcakes are so fantastic, they inspired a haiku . . .

Strawberry shortcake
Sixty-eight calories, WOW!
Will you marry me?

Ingredients

¾ cup angel food cake mix (⅓ of a 16-ounce box)
¾ cup Cool Whip Free, thawed
¾ cup sugar-free strawberry preserves
¾ cup sliced fresh strawberries

Directions

Preheat oven to 375 degrees.

Line a 12-cup muffin pan with baking cups. (You MUST use baking cups for this recipe.) Do not spray with nonstick spray.

Place cake mix in a medium mixing bowl. Add ½ cup water. Using an electric mixer, beat at low speed for 30 seconds. Increase speed to medium and mix for 1 minute. Let sit for 2 minutes.

Evenly distribute cake mixture among baking cups. Bake in the oven for 12 to 15 minutes, until tops are golden brown.

Allow cupcakes to cool completely, then carefully peel cupcakes from baking cups and plate them. Spread 1 tablespoon preserves over the top of each cupcake. Top each with 1 tablespoon Cool Whip. Evenly distribute sliced strawberries among the cupcake tops. Yay!

MAKES 12 SERVINGS

jelly-filled cupcakes

PER SERVING (1 cupcake): 92 calories, 1.75g fat, 155mg sodium, 19g carbs, 0g fiber, 9.5g sugars, 0.5g protein

Yum! Eat one of these moist little cupcakes, and you, too, will be jelly-filled.

Ingredients

2 cups moist-style yellow cake mix (½ of an 18.25-ounce box)
⅓ cup no-sugar-added applesauce
¼ cup sugar-free strawberry preserves
½ teaspoon baking powder

Directions

Preheat oven to 350 degrees.

In a large mixing bowl, combine cake mix and baking powder. Add applesauce and 1 cup water, then stir until blended.

Spray a 12-cup muffin pan with nonstick spray. Evenly distribute cake mixture among the cups. Bake in the oven for 20 to 22 minutes, until a toothpick inserted into the center of a cupcake comes out clean.

Meanwhile, place preserves in the bottom corner of a large plastic bag. Snip the corner off with scissors. This will be used to pipe the preserves into the cupcakes.

Remove cupcakes from the oven. Use a knife to carefully poke a small hole right in the middle of the top of each cupcake. Use the baggie to squeeze the preserves evenly into the holes you created in the cupcakes. Allow to cool completely, then enjoy!

MAKES 12 SERVINGS

HG Tip! Feel free to experiment with your favorite flavors of sugar-free preserves.

blueberry-packed lemon shorties

These are short and sweet . . . literally!

Ingredients

For Cupcakes
2 cups moist-style lemon cake mix (½ of an 18.25-ounce box)
1 cup diet lemon-lime soda
¾ cup fresh blueberries, divided
¼ cup fat-free liquid egg substitute
1 teaspoon baking powder

For Frosting
1 cup Cool Whip Free, thawed
½ cup skim milk
2 tablespoons sugar-free fat-free lemon instant pudding mix

Optional Topping
12 additional blueberries

Directions

Preheat oven to 350 degrees.

To make frosting, combine pudding mix and skim milk in a medium mixing bowl. Using an electric mixer set to medium speed, mix for 1 to 2 minutes. Let sit for 5 minutes. Mix in Cool Whip and refrigerate until cupcakes are ready to be frosted.

In a large mixing bowl, combine cake mix, soda, egg substitute, and baking powder. Stir until blended and lump-free.

Spray a 12-cup muffin pan with nonstick spray. Evenly distribute cake mixture among the cups.

Place half of the blueberries on top of the cake mixture in the cups, about 3 to 4 blueberries each. Bake in the oven for 8 minutes.

Remove pan from the oven and evenly distribute remaining blueberries among cups, pressing down slightly to keep the berries from rolling. Return pan to the oven and bake for an additional 7 minutes, or until cupcake edges are slightly browned.

Let cupcakes cool completely, then evenly distribute frosting among the tops. Add a blueberry to the top of each cupcake, if you like. Refrigerate until ready to serve. Lemon-licious!

MAKES 12 SERVINGS

Chew on This

Blueberries were very important to northeastern Native American tribes; the berries were often used as medicine. They're also great in cupcakes!

banana cupcakes with pb frosting

PER SERVING (1 frosted cupcake): 143 calories, 3.75g fat, 193mg sodium, 25g carbs, 0.5g fiber, 13g sugars, 2g protein

It's a rare combo in cupcake-land—banana and peanut butter! Pssst ... the frosting is SOOOOO peanut buttery!

Ingredients

HG Heads Up! These are best the day they are prepared.

For Cupcakes
2 cups moist-style yellow cake mix (½ of an 18.25-ounce box)
1 large banana, mashed
⅓ cup Gerber bananas (or another brand of pureed bananas found in the baby foods aisle)
½ teaspoon baking powder

For Frosting
¾ cup Cool Whip Free, thawed
¼ cup reduced-fat peanut butter, room temperature

Optional Topping
12 slices banana

Directions

Preheat oven to 375 degrees.

In a small mixing bowl, combine peanut butter and Cool Whip, stirring until mixed well. Refrigerate until cupcakes are ready to be frosted.

In a large mixing bowl, combine cake mix with baking powder and 1 cup water until mixed well. Add pureed bananas and stir thoroughly. Mix in mashed banana.

Line a 12-cup muffin pan with baking cups and/or spray with nonstick spray. Evenly distribute cake mixture among the cups.

Bake in the oven for about 20 minutes, until a toothpick inserted into the center of a cupcake comes out clean.

Once cupcakes have cooled completely, spread frosting evenly over the cupcake tops. Top each cupcake with a slice of banana, if you like. Refrigerate until ready to serve.

MAKES 12 SERVINGS

For Weight Watchers *POINTS*®
values and photos of all the
recipes in this book, check out
hungry-girl.com/book.

chapter ten

sweet stuff

Desserts, Snacks, and Treats

Yee-haaaa! Custards, puddings, pies, cakes, tartlets, snack mixes, and more. This chapter is overflowing with completely delicious, sweet dessert items. Not gonna waste a second more of your time on the setup. You get the idea. Now dive in and whip up some of these head-explodingly good treats!

104-calorie crème brûlée

PER SERVING (1 custard cup): 104 calories, 0.5g fat, 126mg sodium, 18.5g carbs, 0g fiber, 17g sugars, 4.5g protein

This recipe was co-developed with the QUEEN of crème brûlée herself, my pal (and crème brûlée cookbook author) Debbie!

Ingredients

⅓ cup fat-free liquid egg substitute

½ cup fat-free evaporated milk

½ cup fat-free half & half

3 tablespoons plus 1 teaspoon brown sugar
  (not packed)

1½ teaspoons Coffee-mate Sugar Free French
  Vanilla powdered creamer

1¼ teaspoons vanilla extract

4 teaspoons granulated white sugar

HG Heads Up!
You can find a cheapie-cheap kitchen torch at places like Bed Bath & Beyond or online. Or just enjoy this delicious custard without the crispy top!

Directions

Preheat oven to 325 degrees.

In a medium unheated pot, combine evaporated milk, half & half, and brown sugar. Bring to medium heat, then stir and cook until the sugar has dissolved and milk mixture is hot. Stir in the powdered creamer, blending well. Remove from heat.

In a large bowl, mix the egg substitute and vanilla extract together. Gradually whisk in the hot milk mixture. Set four 4-ounce baking ramekins or custard cups in a deep baking dish. Evenly distribute the custard mixture among the cups.

Carefully pour hot water into the baking dish, around the cups, being careful not to splash any water into the custards (or on yourself!). The water should come about halfway up the outsides of the custard cups. Carefully transfer pan to the oven and bake for about 28 minutes, until custards are set.

Remove custard cups from the oven, allow to cool, and then refrigerate until completely chilled, about 2 hours.

Once ready to serve, top each custard cup with 1 teaspoon white sugar. Using a hand-held butane kitchen torch, caramelize the sugar (in other words, blast it with fire 'til browned).

MAKES 4 SERVINGS

super-duper
strawberry shortcake

PER SERVING (entire dessert): 191 calories, 2g fat, 172mg sodium, 41.5g carbs, 2g fiber, 20.5g sugars, 3.5g protein

Since strawberry shortcake is so good, there are THREE fabulous s-berry shortcake recipes in this book. This one has ice cream, there's a cupcake version (page 222), and we've even got a frozen bite-sized variety (page 256). They're all reeeeally good . . . so ENJOY!

Ingredients

1 shortcake dessert shell
⅓ cup sliced strawberries
⅓ cup fat-free vanilla ice cream
2 tablespoons Fat Free Reddi-wip
1 tablespoon sugar-free strawberry preserves

Directions

In a small dish, combine preserves with ½ tablespoon hot water. Mix well to make a strawberry sauce and set aside.

Place one-third of the sliced strawberries in the center of the shortcake. Top with ice cream.

Place another third of the strawberries over the ice cream. (If you want to be all fancy, press the berry slices into the ice cream.) Drizzle strawberry sauce on top.

Squirt your dessert with Reddi-wip and top with remaining strawberries. (Again, feel free to get swanky and arrange the fruit prettily around the whipped topping.)

MAKES 1 SERVING

tiramisu pudding

PER SERVING (entire dessert): 166 calories, 1g fat, 297mg sodium, 24g carbs, 0g fiber, 7g sugars, 14g protein

A few key ingredients, a few swirls of a spoon, and—voilà—you've got tiramisu-flavored pudding. Yes!

Ingredients

½ cup fat-free ricotta cheese

One-half Jell-O Sugar Free Vanilla Pudding Snack

¼ cup Cool Whip Free, thawed

2 tablespoons Splenda No Calorie Sweetener (granulated)

¼ teaspoon vanilla extract

¼ teaspoon unsweetened cocoa powder

Directions

In your favorite dessert bowl, combine ricotta cheese, pudding, Cool Whip, Splenda, and vanilla extract. Stir until smooth.

Sprinkle with cocoa powder. Dig in!

MAKES 1 SERVING

top banana bread

PER SERVING (⅛th of recipe): 140 calories, 0.5g fat, 267mg sodium, 31g carbs, 3.75g fiber, 7g sugars, 5g protein

I never EVER thought I could eat banana bread without downing an insane amount of fat and calories. This recipe is pretty amazing because you get a nice FAT CHUNK of sweet banana bread for not a lot of calories—and it has almost 4 grams of fiber to boot!

Ingredients

1¼ cups whole-wheat flour

¼ cup all-purpose flour

¾ cup Splenda No Calorie Sweetener (granulated)

1½ cups mashed ripe bananas (about 3 bananas)

½ cup fat-free liquid egg substitute

½ cup no-sugar-added applesauce

2 teaspoons baking powder

1 teaspoon vanilla extract

½ teaspoon cinnamon

½ teaspoon salt

Optional toppings: I Can't Believe It's Not Butter! Spray, Cool Whip Free

Directions

Preheat oven to 350 degrees.

In a large mixing bowl, combine both types of flour, Splenda, baking powder, cinnamon, and salt (in other words, all the dry ingredients). Mix well.

In a medium mixing bowl, combine mashed bananas, egg substitute, applesauce, and vanilla extract (all the wet ingredients). Mix thoroughly. Add the wet mixture to the bowl containing the dry ingredients and stir until just blended.

Spoon batter into a large loaf pan (about 9 inches by 5 inches) sprayed with nonstick spray. Bake for about 50 minutes, or until a knife inserted into the middle of the loaf comes out clean.

Allow the loaf to cool slightly, then cut into eight slices. Spritz with some spray butter or spread on some Cool Whip Free just before serving, if you like. YUM!

MAKES 8 SERVINGS

📷 For a pic of this recipe, see the second photo insert. Yay!

Chew on This

The average slice of banana bread contains a ridiculous 326 calories and 12 grams fat, and it's not uncommon for a slice to have TWICE as much fat as that (thanks to all those nuts!). That's BANANAS!

"swirls gone wild" cheesecake brownies

Not only are these delicious, they're also kinda pretty!

Ingredients

One 18.25-ounce box devil's food cake mix

One 15-ounce can pure pumpkin

6 ounces fat-free cream cheese, room temperature

¼ cup Splenda No Calorie Sweetener (granulated)

1 teaspoon Coffee-mate Sugar Free French Vanilla powdered creamer

¼ teaspoon vanilla extract

Directions

Preheat oven to 400 degrees.

In a large mixing bowl, combine cake mix and pumpkin, stirring until completely blended. Batter will be very thick.

Spray a large baking pan (about 9 inches by 13 inches) with nonstick spray. Spread batter into the pan and set aside.

Place powdered creamer in a medium mixing bowl. Add 2 tablespoons warm water and stir until creamer has dissolved.
Add cream cheese, Splenda, and vanilla extract.
Using a whisk, mix vigorously until completely blended, smooth, and lump-free.

Spoon cheesy mixture over the brownie batter and use a knife to swirl it in. Don't worry if your swirl isn't perfect—your brownies will taste delicious no matter what!

Bake in the oven for 20 to 25 minutes, until a knife inserted into the center comes out clean. Allow brownies to cool completely. Cut into sixteen pieces. Enjoy!

MAKES 16 SERVINGS

For a pic of this recipe, see the second photo insert. Yay!

HG Fast Fact:

Rumor has it, a slice of Brownie Sundae Cheesecake at the Cheesecake Factory contains 970 calories and 63 grams fat. THAT is brownie insanity!

gooey crunch fruit tartlets

PER SERVING (2 fruit tartlets): 86 calories, 1g fat, 120mg sodium, 18g carbs, 2g fiber, 6g sugars, 2g protein

These tartlets are sweet, fruity, gooey, and crispy all at the same time. They're also a great little party dessert . . .

Ingredients

For Fruit Filling

1½ cups strawberries, halved if large

1½ cups peeled peach slices

2 tablespoons Splenda No Calorie Sweetener (granulated)

2 tablespoons cornstarch

¼ teaspoon cinnamon

¼ teaspoon vanilla extract

Dash salt

For Tartlets

12 small square wonton wrappers (found with the refrigerated Asian items in the supermarket)

48 sprays I Can't Believe It's Not Butter! Spray

Optional Toppings

Fat Free Reddi-wip

Splenda No Calorie Sweetener (granulated)

Directions

In a small dish, combine Splenda, cornstarch, cinnamon, vanilla extract, and salt. Add ½ cup cold water and stir until ingredients have dissolved.

Set a medium pot sprayed with nonstick spray over medium-low heat. Add strawberries and peaches, then cover with the liquid mixture from the previous step.

Stirring continuously, cook until liquid mixture becomes uniform, thick, and syrupy. Transfer fruit filling to a storage container and let cool slightly. Refrigerate until completely chilled.

Preheat oven to 350 degrees. Spray a 12-cup muffin pan with nonstick spray and set aside.

On a clean dry surface, set out four wonton wrappers. Spray each with two sprays of I Can't Believe It's Not Butter! and use your fingers to spread butter spray evenly over each wonton. Gently flip wontons and repeat. Carefully transfer wontons to the muffin pan, placing each in a muffin cup and pressing it in to form a cup shape. Repeat process with remaining wonton wrappers.

Bake wonton cups in the oven for 10 minutes, or until firm and brown. Once cool enough to handle, transfer wonton cups to a plate and allow to cool completely.

When it's time to serve, evenly spoon chilled fruit filling into the wonton cups. Top each tartlet with a squirt of Reddi-wip or a sprinkling of Splenda, if desired. Enjoy immediately!

MAKES 6 SERVINGS

For Weight Watchers **POINTS**®
values and photos of all the
recipes in this book, check out
hungry-girl.com/book.

mini microwave
triple chocolate cake

PER SERVING (entire dessert): 130 calories, 1.5g fat,
202mg sodium, 27g carbs, 0.5g fiber, 16.5g sugars, 1.5g protein

*Don't like making huge cakes for fear you'll devour several servings at once?
This little chocolate cake dessert is PERFECT for you!*

○ Ingredients

2 tablespoons devil's food cake mix
2 tablespoons Cool Whip Free, thawed
1 tablespoon fat-free vanilla yogurt
1 tablespoon Hershey's Lite chocolate syrup, divided

○ Directions

In a small dish, stir together Cool Whip and half of the chocolate syrup. Place chocolatey whipped topping in the freezer to firm up while you prep the rest of your dessert.

In a very small microwave-safe dish (like a ramekin), combine cake mix and yogurt. Stir until smooth and blended. Don't worry if it seems like a small amount. Your cake will puff up as it cooks—we promise!

Microwave for 1 minute. Allow to cool for 5 minutes.

Remove chocolatey whipped topping from the freezer and spoon it over your cake. Drizzle the remaining chocolate syrup on top. Enjoy!

MAKES 1 SERVING

HG Trivia Tidbit:

Back in 1946, smarty-pants scientist Dr. Percy Spencer came up with the idea for the microwave oven. When the first one hit the market in '47, it was 5½ feet tall, weighed more than 750 pounds, and cost about $5,000. Not exactly a household staple . . .

cran-tastic baked pear slices

PER SERVING (¼th of recipe): 98 calories, 0g fat, 20mg sodium, 26g carbs, 5g fiber, 17g sugars, 0.5g protein

These are crazy-simple to make and can be served as a dessert or tasty side dish.

Ingredients

4 medium pears, sliced
1½ cups Diet Ocean Spray Cranberry Spray
Dash cinnamon

Directions

Preheat oven to 375 degrees.

Spray a large baking dish lightly with nonstick spray. Lay pear slices flat in the dish. Sprinkle with cinnamon and pour cranberry drink on top.

Bake in the oven for 45 minutes, or until pear slices are soft.

Remove from the oven and let pears sit in the "juice" for at least 30 minutes.

Drain any excess liquid from pears. Enjoy hot, cold, or anywhere in between!

MAKES 4 SERVINGS

Chew on This

Of all fruits, pears are one of the least allergenic. Verrrry interesting!

"it's a snap!" ginger cookie 'n peach parfait

PER SERVING (entire parfait): 158 calories, 2.5g fat, 285mg sodium, 33.5g carbs, 1.25g fiber, 13.5g sugars, 2g protein

Gingersnaps, peaches, pudding, and whipped cream?!
No need for any more info here, people.

Ingredients

1 Jell-O Sugar Free Vanilla Pudding Snack
2 gingersnaps, crushed
½ cup diced peaches
2 tablespoons Fat Free Reddi-wip

Directions

Spoon half of the pudding into a parfait glass or small bowl. Top with half of the peaches.

Sprinkle half of the crushed cookies over the peaches. Top with remaining pudding.

Add the rest of the peaches to your parfait. Top with remaining crushed cookies. Finish off with Reddi-wip and enjoy!

MAKES 1 SERVING

Chew on This

Ginger gets its name from the Sanskrit word *"stringa-vera,"* which means "with a body like a horn." In other words, this herb looks like antlers. Attractive!

pb & j cocoa-nana snack mix

PER SERVING (¾ cup): 110 calories, 2g fat, 132mg sodium, 22g carbs, 1g fiber, 12g sugars, 2g protein

You'll go cuckoo for this peanut-buttery, strawberry-licious, chocolate-banana mix. Weeeee!

Ingredients

2 Nature Valley Peanut Butter Crunchy Granola Bars (1 pack)
¾ cup Cocoa Puffs cereal (original)
2 servings (about 1 cup) Gerber Finger Foods Banana Fruit Puffs
1 cup freeze-dried strawberries

Directions

Break granola bars into small bite-sized pieces.

Place granola pieces along with all of the other ingredients in a sealable plastic bag or an airtight container with a lid. Secure, shake well to mix, and enjoy!

MAKES 4 SERVINGS

Chew on This

Trail mixes were created for outdoor activities like hiking, camping, and mountain-climbing—and a typical serving is just 3 to 4 tablespoons. Our snack mixes were created for hungry people who love to eat fun food combos by the handful.

so-good chocolate chip softies

PER SERVING (1 softie): 88 calories, 1.5g fat, 93mg sodium, 17g carbs, 2g fiber, 6g sugars, 3g protein

There's a big debate going on at the HG HQ about these. Are they big soft cookies or muffin tops? We decided to call 'em "softies" and just accept them. We're still not sure exactly what they are, other than delicious!

Ingredients

¾ cup whole-wheat flour

½ cup Splenda No Calorie Sweetener (granulated)

6 tablespoons no-sugar-added applesauce

¼ cup canned pure pumpkin

¼ cup fat-free liquid egg substitute

2½ tablespoons mini semi-sweet chocolate chips

2 tablespoons brown sugar (not packed)

¾ teaspoon vanilla extract

¼ teaspoon baking soda

⅛ teaspoon salt

Directions

Preheat oven to 375 degrees.

In a large mixing bowl, combine all of the dry ingredients except for the chocolate chips (flour, Splenda, brown sugar, baking soda, and salt). Mix well.

In a medium mixing bowl, stir together all of the wet ingredients (applesauce, pumpkin, egg substitute, and vanilla extract).

Add wet mixture to the dry ingredients in the large bowl. Stir until completely blended. Fold in the chocolate chips.

Spray a large baking sheet with nonstick spray. Spoon batter into eight evenly spaced circles. Bake in the oven for about 10 minutes, until softies appear fully cooked and feel firm.

Allow to cool slightly. But for best results, enjoy while still warm!

MAKES 8 SERVINGS

HG Trivia Tidbit:

Chocolate had been enjoyed as a drink for centuries in ancient civilizations before Spanish explorers brought it back to Europe. No big surprise that it caught on! But it wasn't until the early 1800s that companies started producing the solid chocolate we know and love today.

For Weight Watchers *POINTS*® values and photos of all the recipes in this book, check out hungry-girl.com/book.

funky monkey squares

PER SERVING (1 square): 73 calories, 1.5g fat, 153mg sodium, 13g carbs, 1g fiber, 7.5g sugars, 1.5g protein

These treats aren't cookies ... they aren't brownies ... they're just insanely delicious baked squares of chocolate-banana fun.

Ingredients

One 25-calorie packet diet hot cocoa mix

1 medium banana, mashed

¼ cup (about 2) egg whites

⅓ cup whole-wheat flour

⅓ cup brown sugar (not packed)

3 tablespoons Splenda No Calorie Sweetener (granulated)

2 tablespoons light whipped butter or light buttery spread

1 tablespoon mini semi-sweet chocolate chips

1 teaspoon baking powder

½ teaspoon vanilla extract

¼ teaspoon salt

Directions

Preheat oven to 325 degrees.

In a glass, add cocoa mix to ¼ cup hot water. Stir until dissolved, then set aside.

In a medium mixing bowl, combine all the remaining dry ingredients except for the mini chocolate chips (flour, brown sugar, Splenda, salt, and baking powder). Mix well and set aside.

Microwave butter in a small dish until melted, then set aside.

In a large mixing bowl, use a fork to lightly beat egg whites for 1 minute. Add melted butter, vanilla extract, and cocoa mixture, and mix thoroughly.

Slowly stir the dry ingredients into the wet ingredients in the large bowl. Mix in mashed banana.

Spray an 8-inch by 8-inch baking dish with nonstick spray. Pour batter into the dish and top evenly with mini chocolate chips.

Bake in the oven for 30 minutes, or until a toothpick inserted into the center comes out clean.

Let cool slightly, then cut into nine squares. Dig in!

MAKES 9 SERVINGS

HG Fast Fact:

Bananas are packed to the peel with potassium, making them super-effective at helping to lower or prevent high blood pressure. A banana a day keeps the cardiologist away.

hungry girl-nola

PER SERVING (about 1 cup): 165 calories, 1.25g fat, 70mg sodium, 35.5g carbs, 4g fiber, 10g sugars, 4g protein

Guilt-free granola—where have you been all my life???

Ingredients

½ cup bite-sized freeze-dried apples
¼ cup regular oats (not instant)
¼ cup puffed wheat cereal
¼ cup puffed rice cereal
1½ tablespoons sugar-free pancake syrup

Directions

Preheat oven to 275 degrees.

In a medium mixing bowl, combine oats, puffed wheat, puffed rice, and pancake syrup, stirring gently to coat the oats and cereal with the syrup.

Spray a baking sheet with nonstick spray and spread the cereal mixture out on the sheet.

Bake in the oven for 30 to 35 minutes, rearranging mixture with a spatula about halfway through. Granola is done when crispy and lightly browned.

Allow to cool completely, then stir in the apples. Dig in!

MAKES 1 SERVING

 For a pic of this recipe, see the second photo insert. Yay!

Chew on This

Many granola recipes call for oil, honey, and lots of shriveled, sugar-coated dried fruit. Ours calls for sugar-free syrup and light, crispy freeze-dried fruit. All those extra calories are REALLY unnecessary.

marshmallow fudge mania!

If you love our Dreamy Chocolate Peanut Butter Fudge (see the first HG book), you'll dig this marshmallow-y version, too. It's even more chocolatey than the first recipe!

Ingredients

One 18.3-ounce box Betty Crocker Fudge Brownies Traditional Chewy Brownie Mix
2 cups canned pure pumpkin
½ cup Jet-Puffed Marshmallow Creme, room temperature, divided
2 tablespoons Hershey's Lite chocolate syrup

Directions

Preheat oven to 350 degrees.

In a large mixing bowl, combine pumpkin with brownie mix and stir until smooth. Add chocolate syrup and stir until blended. Batter will be very thick, but don't add anything else!

Spray a square baking pan (9-inch by 9-inch works best) with nonstick spray. Spread half the batter into the pan. Spoon half of the marshmallow creme on top and use a knife to swirl it around the top of the batter.

Spread the remaining brownie batter evenly over the top. Then spoon the rest of the marshmallow creme on top and again use a knife to swirl it around.

Bake in the oven for 35 minutes. Batter will remain very thick and fudgy and it should look undercooked.

Allow fudge to cool, then cover pan with foil and refrigerate for at least 2 hours. Cut into thirty-six squares. Then get ready for a fudge frenzy!

MAKES 36 SERVINGS

HG Trivia Tidbit:

The true fudge fanatics flock to northern Michigan each year for the annual Mackinac Island Fudge Festival. "Fudgies"—local slang for the treat-happy tourists—enjoy the Fudge Festival Dance Series, meals Under the Influence (of fudge!), and, of course, enough fudge to last 'til next year's festival. Craziness!

fruity vanilla snack mix

PER SERVING (1 cup): 103 calories, 1.5g fat, 70mg sodium, 21.5g carbs, 1.5g fiber, 16.5g sugars, 1g protein

OMG! This snack mix is really fantastic. It's chewy, crunchy, fruity, and vanilla-licious all at once!

Ingredients

3 cups popped 94 percent fat-free kettle corn microwave popcorn
1 cup bite-sized freeze-dried apples
4 full-sized (or 13 mini) vanilla meringue cookies
¼ cup dried apricots, chopped
2 tablespoons All Natural Almond Accents in Butter Toffee Glazed or Honey Roasted

Directions

Break meringues into small pieces.

In a sealable plastic bag or an airtight container with a lid, combine meringue pieces with all of the other ingredients. Secure bag or container and shake thoroughly. Now go nuts!

MAKES 4 SERVINGS

HG Trivia Tidbit:

This recipe uses meringues, which are sometimes called "forgotten cookies," simply because you bake them for an hour and then let them sit in the cooling oven for at least another hour—or until you remember that you have fresh crispy cookies waiting for you.

chewy s'mores snack mix

PER SERVING (¾ cup): 109 calories, 1.25g fat, 103mg sodium, 23.5g carbs, 0.5g fiber, 13.5g sugars, 0.5g protein

The Tootsie Rolls ROCK in this fun recipe! Try it and see.

Ingredients

2 cups popped 94 percent fat-free kettle corn microwave popcorn
1 cup Golden Grahams cereal
¾ cup Cocoa Puffs cereal (original)
¾ cup mini marshmallows
10 Tootsie Roll Midgees

Directions

Chop Tootsie Roll Midgees into very small pieces.

In a sealable plastic bag or an airtight container with a lid, combine Tootsie Roll pieces with all of the other ingredients. Secure bag or container and shake thoroughly.

MAKES 6 SERVINGS

HG Trivia Tidbit:

The first mention of s'mores showed up in a Girl Scouts handbook in 1927. The recipe is credited to Loretta Scott Crew, who made them for a legion of hungry Girl Scouts by the campfire. Loretta TOTALLY earned her patch for cooking!

chapter eleven

fun with
cool whip free

A Fluffy Good Time

Yes, there's an entire chapter dedicated to recipes made with Cool Whip Free. If you're opposed to the stuff in any way, shape, or form, and you don't want to take part in the celebration of its fluffy fat-free goodness, feel free to move on. If, however, you're bold enough to appreciate Cool Whip Free in moderation and in various states (I mean frozen or thawed—not Montana or New Jersey!), you'll FLIP over this chapter and its glorious recipes. Love it or leave it!

mmmm! miracle mousse

PER SERVING (entire dessert): 100 calories, 2.5g fat, 195mg sodium, 21g carbs, 0.5g fiber, 2.5g sugars, 1.5g protein

This two-ingredient mousse can be made in a bazillion flavors. Just pick your pudding of choice and have fun!

⊙ Ingredients

1 Jell-O Sugar Free Pudding Snack (any flavor)
⅓ cup Cool Whip Free, thawed

⊙ Directions

Simply combine the pudding and Cool Whip in your favorite dessert bowl and mix well.

Enjoy your fantastically fluffy 100-calorie dessert. Woohoo!

MAKES 1 SERVING

HG Fast Fact:

The plural form of the word "moose" is "moose." The plural form of the word "mouse" is "mice." The plural form of the word "mousse" is "mousses." Discuss.

toffee almond caramel cream cakes

PER SERVING (6 cream cakes): 96 calories, 3.5g fat, 121mg sodium, 12.5g carbs, 0.25g fiber, 4g sugars, 2.5g protein

Here's a simple little recipe that'll kick a craving for crunch, sweets, and ice cream, too. And you get to eat SIX of these babies . . .

Ingredients

6 caramel soy crisps or mini rice cakes
2 tablespoons Cool Whip Free, thawed
1 tablespoon All Natural Almond Accents in Butter Toffee Glazed, crushed

Directions

Place soy crisps or mini rice cakes on a plate and spread 1 teaspoon Cool Whip over each. Sprinkle crushed almonds evenly over whipped topping.

Freeze until the tops are cold and solid, about 1 hour. Store in the freezer until ready to serve. Gobble 'em up!

MAKES 1 SERVING

HG Tip! These taste best within a day or so of making them. After that, they'll need to be slightly thawed before eating.

strawberry shortcake bites

PER SERVING (2 shortcake bites): 88 calories, 1g fat,
128mg sodium, 21g carbs, 0g fiber, 4g sugars, <1g protein

Chilly, fruity, sweet snack bites with a surprising CRUNCH on the bottom . . .

Ingredients

1 Jell-O Sugar Free Vanilla Pudding Snack
⅓ cup Cool Whip Free, thawed
2 tablespoons sugar-free strawberry preserves
4 Reduced Fat Nilla Wafers

Directions

In a small bowl, combine pudding, Cool Whip, and preserves. Mix well and set aside.

Place four baking cups on a plate or in four cups of a muffin pan. Put one wafer in each baking cup. Spoon one-fourth of the pudding mixture on top of each wafer.

Freeze until solid, about 1 hour. Store in the freezer until ready to serve.

MAKES 2 SERVINGS

HG Tip! These taste best within a day or so of making them. After that, they'll need to be slightly thawed before eating.

caramel piña colada crunchers

PER SERVING (2 crunchers): 90 calories, 0.5g fat, 98mg sodium, 20g carbs, 1g fiber, 8g sugars, <1g protein

These are pretty awesome—they're creamy little frozen nuggets crammed with caramel, pineapple, coconut, and more. Yum!

Ingredients

2 Jell-O Sugar Free Vanilla Pudding Snacks
One-half 8-ounce container Cool Whip Free, thawed
One 8-ounce can crushed pineapple in juice, lightly drained
½ cup Fiber One Caramel Delight cereal
½ teaspoon coconut extract
2 no-calorie sweetener packets

Directions

Place cereal in a medium mixing bowl and lightly crush. Add all of the other ingredients and mix well.

Line a 12-cup muffin pan with baking cups and spray with nonstick spray. Evenly distribute pudding mixture among the cups.

Freeze until solid, about 1 hour. Store in the freezer until ready to serve. Crunch it up!

MAKES 6 SERVINGS

Chew on This

According to urban legend, falling coconuts kill ten times as many people as shark attacks. We're pretty sure coconut extract never gave anyone a concussion!

HG Tip! These taste best within a day or so of making them. After that, they'll need to be slightly thawed before eating.

pb-nana poppers

PER SERVING (5 poppers): 108 calories, 3g fat, 57mg sodium, 18.5g carbs, 2g fiber, 8.5g sugars, 2.5g protein

AHHHHHH! These little frozen banana sandwiches are too cute—and REALLY tasty!

☐ Ingredients

1 medium-large banana
2 tablespoons Cool Whip Free, thawed
1 tablespoon reduced-fat peanut butter, room temperature

☐ Directions

Cut banana into twenty circular slices. Lay ten slices flat on a plate and set all of the banana slices aside.

In a small bowl, mix Cool Whip and peanut butter until blended. Evenly distribute PB mixture on top of the banana slices on the plate.

Finish off by placing another banana slice on top of each covered slice, making 10 mini sandwiches.

Freeze until solid, about 1 hour. Store in the freezer until ready to serve. Enjoy!

MAKES 2 SERVINGS

HG Tip! Eat or serve these within a day or so of making them. After that, they'll need to be slightly thawed before eating.

For Weight Watchers **POINTS®** values and photos of all the recipes in this book, check out hungry-girl.com/book.

Crazy Calypso Salad, p. 139

Mini Meal Mania

Crazy-Good Coconut Chicken Taco, p. 148

Philly Cheesesteak Lettuce Cups, p. 155

Smothered Pig in a Blanket, p. 141

So Low Mein with Chicken, p. 142

BBQ Mango Tilapia, p. 144

Chicken Fajita Lettuce Cups, p. 146

Cheesy Saucy Veggie Stacks, p. 158

Tortilla Madness

Little Taco Salad in a Shell, p. 184

Spicy Tortilla Pizza Mexicali, p. 178

Cheeseburger Quesadilla, p. 182

Raspberry Mocha Madness Swappuccino, p. 191

Cravin' Cap'n Crunch Shake, p. 189

Key Lime Pie Shake, p. 201

Yo, Cupcake!

Red Velvet Insanity Cupcakes, p. 208

Chocolate Marshmallow Madness Cupcakes, p. 212

Crazy-Crumbly Super-Yummy Coffee Cakes, p. 206

Death by Chocolate Cone Cakes, p. 218

Sweet Stuff

Top Banana Bread, p. 234

Hungry Girl-nola, p. 248

"Swirls Gone Wild" Cheesecake Brownies, p. 236

Fun with Cool Whip Free, Fujis, Fiber One, and Vitalicious

Sweet Cinnamon Fritter Fries, p. 288

Double-Trouble Chocolate Trifle, p. 323

Red Hot Apple Pie in a Cup, p. 272

Gimme Gimme S'mores Sandwich, p. 260

chunky & nutty frozen pb cups

PER SERVING (1 pb cup): 78 calories, 2g fat, 123mg sodium, 11.5g carbs, 0.5g fiber, 2.5g sugars, 2g protein

Peanut butter cups are on pretty much everyone's list of weaknesses. Here's a version for creamy, crunchy, frozen ones that have just 78 calories each!

Ingredients

1 small (4-serving) package sugar-free fat-free chocolate instant pudding mix
One 8-ounce container Cool Whip Free, thawed
2 ounces (about ½ cup) dry-roasted soy nuts
1 tablespoon mini semi-sweet chocolate chips
1 tablespoon reduced-fat peanut butter, room temperature

Directions

Place pudding mix in a medium bowl. Add 3 ounces (¼ cup plus 2 tablespoons) warm water. Stir until smooth and thickened, about 2 minutes.

In a small bowl, combine 1 tablespoon Cool Whip with peanut butter until mixed well. Stir into the pudding mixture.

Stir in half of the soy nuts and all of the mini chocolate chips. Fold in remaining Cool Whip. You don't need to mix it in completely—the marble effect is cool.

Line a 12-cup muffin pan with baking cups and spray with nonstick spray. Evenly distribute pudding mixture among the cups. Sprinkle the tops of the cups with remaining soy nuts.

Freeze until solid, about 1 hour. Store in the freezer until ready to serve.

MAKES 12 SERVINGS

HG Tip! Eat or serve these within a day or so of making them. After that, they'll need to be slightly thawed before eating.

gimme gimme s'mores sandwich

PER SERVING (entire sandwich): 133 calories, 2.5g fat,
99mg sodium, 26g carbs, 0.5g fiber, 11.5g sugars, 1g protein

Ooooh . . . a frozen s'mores sandwich. Fun, fun, FUN!

Ingredients

1 sheet (4 crackers) low-fat honey graham crackers
¼ cup Cool Whip Free, thawed
1 teaspoon mini semi-sweet chocolate chips
8 miniature marshmallows

Directions

In a small bowl, lightly stir together Cool Whip, chocolate chips, and marshmallows.
Don't over-stir.

Break graham cracker sheet into two squares. Place one square on a plate and top
with Cool Whip mixture. Lightly place the other square on top.

Freeze until solid, about 1 hour. Store in the freezer until ready to serve. Enjoy!

MAKES 1 SERVING

 For a pic of this recipe, see the second photo insert. Yay!

HG Trivia Tidbit:

In the old days, marshmallows were made from a plant that was
ACTUALLY called a marsh mallow. These days they're comprised of
sugary sweet stuff . . . and no plants at all!

pumpkin pudding parfait

PER SERVING (entire parfait): 172 calories, 2.25g fat,
266mg sodium, 38g carbs, 6g fiber, 7.5g sugars, 3g protein

*Fiber One Caramel Delight cereal makes the combo of pumpkin,
pudding, and whipped topping even BETTER!*

Ingredients

1 Jell-O Sugar Free Vanilla Pudding Snack
½ cup canned pure pumpkin
¼ cup Fiber One Caramel Delight cereal, lightly crushed
2 tablespoons Cool Whip Free, thawed
¼ teaspoon pumpkin pie spice
2 no-calorie sweetener packets
Dash cinnamon
Optional toppings: Fat Free Reddi-wip, additional cinnamon

Directions

In a small bowl, combine pumpkin, Cool Whip,
pumpkin pie spice, sweetener, and cinnamon until
mixed well. Refrigerate until cold.

Place one-third of the pudding in the bottom of a
parfait glass. Top with half of the pumpkin mixture.

Layer another third of the pudding over the pumpkin.
Sprinkle half of the crushed cereal on top.

Complete the parfait by layering the remaining
pumpkin, pudding, and, lastly, cereal. Top it off with
a squirt of Reddi-wip and a sprinkle of
cinnamon, if you like. Consume immediately!

MAKES 1 SERVING

chocolate cherry crunchers

PER SERVING (2 crunchers): 79 calories, 1.5g fat, 67mg sodium, 16g carbs, 1g fiber, 6g sugars, 1g protein

Chocolatey, creamy, frozen cherry-liciousness!

Ingredients

One-half 8-ounce container Cool Whip Free, thawed
2 Jell-O Sugar Free Double Chocolate Pudding Snacks
1 cup frozen unsweetened pitted dark sweet cherries, slightly thawed
1 tablespoon mini semi-sweet chocolate chips

Directions

In a medium mixing bowl, combine all of the ingredients until mixed well.

Line a 12-cup muffin pan with baking cups and spray with nonstick spray. Evenly distribute mixture among the cups.

Freeze until solid, about 1 hour. Devour!

MAKES 6 SERVINGS

HG Tip! These taste best within a day or so of making them. After that, they'll need to be slightly thawed before eating.

Chew on This

Many kinds of cherries are grown all over the U.S. There's Bing, Brooks, King, Rainier, Tulare, Royal Ann, and Evans. Put 'em together and they sound like the characters in a romance novel—Bing Brooks! King Rainier Tulare! Royal Ann Evans!

vanilla-thrilla coffee float

PER SERVING (entire float): 111 calories, 3g fat, 111mg sodium, 17.5g carbs, 0g fiber, 6.5g sugars, 3g protein

Adding a scoop of frozen Cool Whip Free to an iced coffee drink is a fun little way to add zazzle without adding too many calories!

Ingredients

½ cup Cool Whip Free, frozen
½ cup light vanilla soymilk, cold
1 teaspoon instant coffee granules
1 teaspoon Coffee-mate Sugar Free French Vanilla
    powdered creamer
1 no-calorie sweetener packet
2 tablespoons sugar-free calorie-free vanilla syrup

Directions

Place coffee, Coffee-mate, and sweetener in a tall glass. Add ¼ cup hot water and stir until ingredients have dissolved.

Add ½ cup cold water, soymilk, and vanilla syrup. Pour mixture into a cocktail shaker and add many ice cubes. Cover and shake for about 1 minute, until the drink is very cold.

Strain drink into a tall glass, and top with the Cool Whip. Enjoy!

MAKES 1 SERVING

HG Trivia Tidbit:

A typical 16-ounce iced vanilla latte contains around 330 calories and 7 grams fat, and it doesn't even come with fun frozen Cool Whip! BO-RING!

crustless banana cream pie

PER SERVING (⅛th of pie): 115 calories, 1.5g fat, 123mg sodium, 23g carbs, 1g fiber, 12.5g sugars, 1.5g protein

This creamy custard "pie" is PACKED with bananas. And you'll never miss the crust!

Ingredients

2 cups plain light soymilk

1 cup Cool Whip Free, thawed

2½ medium bananas, divided

¼ cup granulated white sugar

¼ cup Splenda No Calorie Sweetener (granulated)

¼ cup cornstarch

1½ tablespoons light whipped butter or light buttery spread

1 teaspoon vanilla extract

¼ teaspoon salt

Directions

In a medium pot, combine sugar, Splenda, cornstarch, and salt.

Place pot over medium-high heat and slowly add soymilk. Stirring constantly with a wire whisk, bring mixture to a boil. Once boiling, continue to stir and cook for 4 minutes.

Remove the pot from heat, and add butter and vanilla extract. Stir until smooth. Allow to cool for 5 minutes. This is your custard mixture.

Slice two bananas into circular slices about ¼-inch thick. In a 9-inch pie dish, layer half the slices along the bottom. Evenly cover with half of the custard mixture.

Layer remaining banana slices on top of the custard. Pour remaining custard mixture over the second banana layer.

Allow to sit at room temperature for about 10 minutes, until slightly cool. Refrigerate for at least 2 hours.

When it's time to serve, spread the Cool Whip over the top of the pie. Cut the remaining half banana into eight circular slices. Evenly arrange the slices around the top of the pie. Cut your crustless pie into eight slices and serve!

MAKES 8 SERVINGS

For Weight Watchers *POINTS*® values and photos of all the recipes in this book, check out hungry-girl.com/book.

chapter twelve

fun with fujis

Things to Do with Apples When You're Bored

Apples are AMAZING. Especially Fujis, which are, hands down, the best kind of apple (just an opinion!). And while it's great to bite right into an apple and enjoy it the old-fashioned way, there are too many other fun ways to celebrate apples. This chapter has apple-tastic desserts, stuffing, a slaw, sides, and more.

jell-o fizzy fruit minis

These mini Jell-O molds are soooooooooooo refreshing and fruity. They're a PERFECT summer dessert but are really fun any time of year.

Ingredients

1 small (4-serving) package Jell-O Sugar Free Raspberry Gelatin Dessert Mix
1¼ cups diet orange soda, cold
½ cup chopped Fuji apples
½ cup chopped peaches or nectarines
Optional topping: Fat Free Reddi-wip

Directions

Place gelatin mix in a medium mixing bowl. Cover with ¾ cup boiling water. Stir constantly for at least 2 minutes, until gelatin has dissolved completely. Stir soda into gelatin mixture. Refrigerate for about 1 hour and 15 minutes, until thickened but not set.

Stir apples and peaches or nectarines into the Jell-O. Evenly distribute mixture among three dessert bowls or small glasses. Return to the fridge until set, about 3 hours longer. Keep refrigerated until ready to serve. If you like, top each mini mold with a squirt of Reddi-wip before digging in!

MAKES 3 SERVINGS

Chew on This

These are WAY better than the boring fruit-in-gelatin concoctions your aunt brings to family get-togethers. (Sorry, aunts across America!)

pico de fuji

This recipe may sound a little weird, but it's actually awesome and really unique—apples, onion, blueberries, jalapeño, and more. Wow!

Ingredients

2 medium Fuji apples, peeled, cored, and diced
1 small lime
1 jalapeño pepper, seeded and diced
¼ cup fresh blueberries
2 tablespoons coarsely chopped fresh cilantro
1 tablespoon diced red onion
¼ teaspoon salt

Directions

Place diced apples in a large bowl. Squeeze the juice from the lime over the apples. Add jalapeño, blueberries, cilantro, onion, and salt. Toss well.

Chill for at least 30 minutes. Keep refrigerated until ready to serve. Enjoy over salads, fish, and chicken, or eat it straight from the bowl!

MAKES 4 SERVINGS

HG Tip! Be VERY careful when handling the jalapeño. Avoid touching your face and eyes, and wash your hands well afterward.

Chew on This

Fuji apples were developed in Fujisaki, Japan, but they're actually a cross between two American apples—Red Delicious and Ralls Genet. We shoulda thought of these first, but thanks, Japan!

fuji fritters

PER SERVING (1 fritter): 93 calories, 1.75g fat, 121mg sodium, 17.5g carbs, 1.5g fiber, 5.5g sugars, 2g protein

These fritters are so good, you may not be able to control yourself around them. No worries, though. You can eat TWO of 'em for less than 200 calories!

Ingredients

For Apple Mixture

3 cups peeled Fuji apple chunks

3 tablespoons Splenda No Calorie Sweetener (granulated)

1 tablespoon cornstarch

1 teaspoon cinnamon

1 teaspoon vanilla extract

For Fritter Base

1⅓ cups regular oats (not instant)

⅔ cup Bisquick Heart Smart baking mix

⅔ cup light vanilla soymilk

2 tablespoons brown sugar (not packed)

1½ tablespoons light whipped butter or light buttery spread

1 teaspoon baking powder

Directions

Preheat oven to 400 degrees.

Place apple chunks in a medium microwave-safe bowl with ¼ cup water. Cover and microwave for 2½ minutes. Once bowl is cool enough to handle, drain water and set aside.

In a medium unheated pot, combine Splenda, cinnamon, vanilla extract, and cornstarch with ½ cup cold water. Cook over medium heat, stirring occasionally. Continue to cook and stir until thickened to a caramel-sauce–like consistency. Remove the pot from heat and stir in apple chunks. Set aside.

In a large mixing bowl, combine all of the ingredients for fritter base until mixed well. Fold apple mixture into the fritter base.

Spray two large baking sheets with nonstick spray. Evenly distribute batter into twelve well-spaced mounds. (The fritters will expand as they cook.)

Bake for 10 to 15 minutes, until a toothpick inserted into the center of a fritter comes out clean. Allow to cool slightly, then enjoy!

MAKES 12 SERVINGS

For Weight Watchers **POINTS**® values and photos of all the recipes in this book, check out hungry-girl.com/book.

red hot apple pie in a cup

PER SERVING (entire recipe): 140 calories, 0.5g fat, 44mg sodium, 47g carbs, 3.5g fiber, 24.5g sugars, 0.5g protein

My good pal "Crème Brûlée" Debbie (see page 230) had the brilliant idea to nuke apples and Red Hots. The more Red Hots you use, the more RED HOT your dessert will be. This recipe is INSANE . . . and a must-try!

Ingredients

1 medium Fuji apple, cored and cubed
12 to 15 pieces Red Hots Cinnamon Flavored Candy
½ sheet (2 crackers) low-fat cinnamon graham crackers, crushed
2 tablespoons Fat Free Reddi-wip
Dash cinnamon

Directions

Place apple cubes in a microwavable cup or mug. Top with Red Hots. Cover and microwave for 2 minutes. Stir well. Microwave for an additional 1 to 2 minutes, until apple cubes are soft.

Once cup or mug is cool enough to handle, mix contents well. Allow to cool for about 10 minutes.

Top with half of the crushed graham crackers followed by the Reddi-wip. Sprinkle with remaining grahams and a little cinnamon. Voilà!

MAKES 1 SERVING

 For a pic of this recipe, see the second photo insert. Yay!

Chew on This

Ahhh, the good old days . . . In the 1800s, rural families considered fruit pies to be a hearty breakfast before a day's work. We typically crave ours AFTER a hard day's work, but we won't tell if you enjoy this one old-school!

i heart apple slaw

PER SERVING (about 1 cup): 59 calories, <0.5g fat, 29.5mg sodium, 13g carbs, 2.5g fiber, 10g sugars, 2g protein

APPLE SLAW = AMAAAAAZING. And it can be a snack, a side dish, or even a dessert. Mmmmmmmmmmmmmm!

Ingredients

1 medium Fuji apple
1 medium Granny Smith apple
2 cups dry broccoli slaw mix
½ cup plain fat-free yogurt
½ tablespoon honey
¾ teaspoon Splenda No Calorie Sweetener (granulated)

Directions

Cut both apples into matchstick-sized strips and place in a large bowl. Add slaw mix to the bowl. Toss well and set aside.

In a small bowl, combine yogurt, honey, and Splenda until mixed well. Pour into the large bowl and stir until apple strips and slaw mix are thoroughly coated.

Chill slaw for at least 30 minutes. Store in the fridge until ready to serve.

MAKES 5 SERVINGS

caramel apple tartlets

PER SERVING (2 tartlets): 100 calories, 2g fat, 76mg sodium, 21g carbs, 1.5g fiber, 11g sugars, 1g protein

Who needs a big honkin' slice of apple pie when you can have one (or several!) of these gooey things?

Ingredients

2½ cups finely chopped Fuji apples

Six 9-inch by 14-inch sheets phyllo dough, thawed according to package directions

¼ cup brown sugar (not packed)

2 tablespoons light whipped butter or light buttery spread, room temperature

1 tablespoon cornstarch

¼ teaspoon cinnamon

Optional topping: Fat Free Reddi-wip

Directions

Preheat oven to 350 degrees.

Immediately after unrolling phyllo sheets, spray with nonstick spray. Divide sheets into two stacks of three. Cut each stack into six sections by cutting each in half lengthwise and then into thirds horizontally. You should now have twelve mini stacks.

Prepare a 12-cup muffin pan by spraying with nonstick spray. Gently place each mini stack into a cup, pressing down lightly with your fingers so the dough creates a cup shape. Bake in the oven for 8 to 10 minutes, until lightly browned. Set aside to cool.

In a small unheated pot, combine butter, brown sugar, cornstarch, and cinnamon with 1 tablespoon water. Stir until ingredients have mostly dissolved.

Over medium heat, cook and stir brown sugar mixture until it thickens to a caramel-sauce–like consistency.

Reduce heat to low and add the apples. Cook for 3 to 4 minutes, until apples have softened, stirring continuously so the filling does not burn.

Evenly distribute filling among the twelve pastry shells. If you like, top with Reddi-wip just before serving. Enjoy hot or cold!

MAKES 6 SERVINGS

HG Fast Fact:

In Western culture, caramel apples are most frequently associated with Halloween and accidental tooth loss. These tartlets are acceptable year-round and risk-free.

apple & onion stuffing

PER SERVING (1 cup): 108 calories, 1g fat, 206mg sodium, 24g carbs, 4.25g fiber, 12g sugars, 3g protein

This sweet stuffing is PERFECT any time of year—but it's ESPECIALLY good on Thanksgiving!

▭ Ingredients

6 slices light bread (40 to 45 calories each with at least 2 grams fiber per slice)
4 cups chopped Fuji apples
2 cups chopped sweet onion
1 cup chopped celery
⅓ cup fat-free chicken broth, room temperature (plus extra if needed)
¼ cup raisins (not packed)
¼ cup minced fresh parsley
¼ cup fat-free liquid egg substitute
1 tablespoon light whipped butter or light buttery spread
1 tablespoon minced shallots
1 teaspoon minced garlic
¼ teaspoon salt
Salt and black pepper, to taste

▭ Directions

Preheat oven to 350 degrees.

Lightly toast bread slices. Cut into cubes and set aside.

Melt butter in a medium pot over medium heat. Once butter has melted, add celery, onion, shallots, garlic, and salt. Sauté veggies for 4 to 5 minutes, stirring frequently.

Remove pot from heat and add apples, raisins, and parsley. Mix well. Add broth and egg substitute, and stir thoroughly.

Spray a medium baking dish with nonstick spray. Transfer veggie mixture from the pot to the baking dish. Add bread cubes and fold in gently. The bread cubes should be moist but not saturated. Add a few extra tablespoons of broth to coat, if needed.

Let stuffing mixture sit at room temperature for several minutes, allowing bread cubes to absorb some of the moisture.

Cover with foil and bake in the oven for 20 minutes. Remove foil and, using a fork, gently fluff and rearrange stuffing. Return to oven, uncovered. Bake for 10 to 15 minutes, until top is golden brown.

While stuffing is still warm, mix gently. Season to taste with salt and pepper. Devour!

MAKES 8 SERVINGS

chunky apple–cinnamon muffins

PER SERVING (1 muffin with topping): 127 calories, 2.5g fat, 325mg sodium, 24.5g carbs, 2.5g fiber, 10g sugars, 3g protein

Stop hiding from muffins, people. Here are straight-up delicious apple-cinnamon muffins you can enjoy guilt-free!

◠ Ingredients

For Muffins

1 cup peeled and chopped Fuji apples
½ cup whole-wheat flour
¼ cup light vanilla soymilk
2 tablespoons sugar-free pancake syrup
2 tablespoons fat-free liquid egg substitute
2 tablespoons Splenda No Calorie Sweetener (granulated)
2 tablespoons brown sugar (not packed)
1½ tablespoons light whipped butter or light buttery spread, room temperature
¾ teaspoon baking powder
½ teaspoon cinnamon
½ teaspoon vanilla extract
¼ teaspoon salt

For Topping

1 tablespoon brown sugar (not packed)
1 teaspoon Splenda No Calorie Sweetener (granulated)
¼ teaspoon cinnamon
½ teaspoon light whipped butter or light buttery spread, room temperature
Dash salt

◠ Directions

Preheat oven to 400 degrees.

In a small mixing bowl, combine all of the ingredients for topping except butter until mixed well. Add butter and gently stir until small crumbs form. Set aside.

In a medium mixing bowl, combine the flour, Splenda, brown sugar, baking powder, cinnamon, and salt for the muffins and mix well.

In a large mixing bowl, combine the soymilk, syrup, egg substitute, butter, and vanilla extract for the muffins. Using a whisk, mix until thoroughly blended. Don't worry if butter bits do not break up completely.

Add the dry muffin ingredients to the large bowl with the wet ingredients. Mix until completely blended, then fold in the apples.

Line four cups of a muffin pan with baking cups and/or spray with nonstick spray. Evenly distribute batter among the four cups. Sprinkle topping mixture evenly over batter in the cups.

Bake in the oven for 18 to 20 minutes, until a toothpick inserted into the center of a muffin comes out clean. Cool slightly before eating. Demolish!

MAKES 4 SERVINGS

For Weight Watchers **POINTS**®
values and photos of all the
recipes in this book, check out
hungry-girl.com/book.

apple icobbler

PER SERVING (about 1 cup): 126 calories, 1g fat, 236mg sodium, 33g carbs, 5.5g fiber, 16g sugars, 2g protein

This cobbler may be crustless, but it does have that sweet, cinnamony, crumbly topping we all know and love. Woohoo!

Ingredients

Heads up, F1 fans! Don't miss our Fun with Fiber One chapter, starting in a couple of pages!

For Apple Mixture

3 cups peeled Fuji apple chunks

2 tablespoons brown sugar (not packed)

1 tablespoon Splenda No Calorie Sweetener (granulated)

1 tablespoon cornstarch

½ teaspoon cinnamon

½ teaspoon vanilla extract

¼ teaspoon salt

For Crumb Topping

2 sheets (8 crackers) low-fat honey graham crackers

½ cup Fiber One bran cereal (original)

2 tablespoons fat-free liquid egg substitute

2 tablespoons no-sugar-added applesauce

2 tablespoons Splenda No Calorie Sweetener (granulated)

1½ teaspoons cinnamon

Directions

Preheat oven to 400 degrees.

In a medium unheated pot, combine all of the apple mixture ingredients except for the apple chunks. Add ⅔ cup cold water and stir well.

Add apple chunks to the pot. Cook over medium heat, stirring occasionally until liquid thickens to a syrupy consistency and begins to bubble. Reduce heat to low and cover. Let simmer for 5 minutes. Transfer mixture to a medium round baking dish and set aside.

Break graham crackers into pieces. Place graham pieces and Fiber One in a blender or food processor. Grind to a breadcrumb-like consistency.

Transfer crumbs to a medium microwave-safe dish. Add all other crumb-topping ingredients and mix well. Microwave for 1 minute.

Use a fork to break up the crumb mixture as much as possible. Allow it to cool for several minutes.

Transfer crumb mixture to the food processor or blender. Pulse until crumbly and uniform. Evenly distribute crumb topping over apple mixture.

Bake in the oven for 10 minutes. Allow cobbler to cool slightly before serving. Chew!

MAKES 4 SERVINGS

HG Fast Fact:

In the U.S., we typically put fruit in our cobblers, but our friends in the U.K. like to fill theirs with meat and veggies. If we have a trans-Atlantic cobbler party, dinner and dessert will be covered.

chapter thirteen

fun with
fiber one

Faux-Frys, Awesome Pies, and More

It's no secret that there's some sort of love affair going on between Hungry Girl and Fiber One cereal. The two have been seen together everywhere—from the blender to the bottom of a pie pan! Here's a roundup of recipes featuring the fiber-infused superstar breakfast cereal.

crispy tuna croquettes

PER SERVING (4 croquettes): 170 calories, 2g fat,
1,059mg sodium, 22g carbs, 10.5g fiber, 0.5g sugars, 25.5g protein

Oh, Fiber One, you never cease to amaze. These croquettes were inspired by one of my favorite TV chefs, Alton Brown.

Ingredients

One 6-ounce can albacore tuna packed in water, drained

¾ cup Fiber One bran cereal (original)

½ cup fat-free liquid egg substitute

2 scallions, finely chopped

2 teaspoons Hellmann's/Best Foods Dijonnaise

1 teaspoon lemon juice

½ teaspoon kosher salt

Optional: additional salt, black pepper

Optional dips: fat-free sour cream,
additional Dijonnaise

Directions

Place Fiber One in a food processor or blender. Add some salt and pepper, if you like. Grind to a breadcrumb-like consistency. Place half of the crumbs in a small dish and set aside.

Place remaining crumbs in a medium mixing bowl. Shred tuna by hand into the bowl. Add scallions, egg substitute, Dijonnaise, salt, and lemon juice. Stir until thoroughly mixed.

Line a large baking sheet with parchment paper. Form tuna mixture into eight mounds on the sheet. Let sit at room temperature for 15 minutes.

Gently coat the mounds in the remaining Fiber One crumbs, making sure to flip them and cover all sides well.

Bring a large pan sprayed with nonstick spray to medium heat on the stove. Cook croquettes for 3 minutes on each side (and not a second less!). Serve with sour cream and extra Dijonnaise for dipping, if you like. Enjoy!

MAKES 2 SERVINGS

Unexpected Fiber Alert!
Fiber in ice cream? Yep. Check out Breyers Double Churn FREE Fat Free Ice Cream. Each cool 'n creamy half-cup scoop serves up 3 to 4 grams fiber.

freakishly fantastic faux-fried zucchini

PER SERVING (⅓rd of recipe): 78 calories, 0.5g fat, 578mg sodium, 20g carbs, 9g fiber, 4g sugars, 5g protein

Fried zucchini is often thought of as a good-for-you option because it involves some sort of green vegetable. Nuh-uh! It's typically greasy and full of fat. Feast your eyes (and taste buds) on our beauteously guilt-free version!

Ingredients

2 large zucchini, ends removed

¾ cup Fiber One bran cereal (original)

¼ cup fat-free liquid egg substitute

1 tablespoon dry ranch dressing/dip mix

¼ teaspoon plus 1 dash garlic powder

¼ teaspoon plus 1 dash onion powder

¼ teaspoon plus 1 dash oregano

2 dashes black pepper

2 dashes salt

Directions

Preheat oven to 350 degrees.

Place Fiber One in a blender or food processor. Add ranch mix and ¼ teaspoon each of garlic powder, onion powder, and oregano. Add a dash each of salt and pepper. Grind to a breadcrumb-like consistency. Transfer crumbs to a medium bowl.

In another medium bowl, combine egg substitute with a dash each of garlic powder, onion powder, oregano, salt, and pepper. Stir thoroughly.

Cut zucchini into ½-inch-wide circles. Blot away any excess moisture with a paper towel.

Spray a large baking sheet with nonstick spray. Toss zucchini circles in seasoned egg substitute until they are all evenly covered. One by one, give zucchini slices a shake to remove excess egg substitute, coat them with breadcrumbs, and lay them flat on the baking sheet.

Bake in the oven for 10 minutes. Carefully flip zucchini slices over. Bake in the oven for 10 additional minutes, or until outsides are crispy and zucchini is cooked through. Yum!

MAKES 3 SERVINGS

HG Fast Fact:

If you order the fried zucchini at Carl's Jr., you'll have to leave a third of those fat-infused fried morsels behind in order to stop at 200 calories. Even then, you'll already have consumed about 12 grams fat!

sweet cinnamon fritter fries

PER SERVING (⅓rd of recipe with syrup): 144 calories, 1g fat, 295mg sodium, 41g carbs, 12g fiber, 3g sugars, 5g protein

When you taste these fries, you'll squeal with delight so uncontrollably that the neighbors may call the cops. So close all doors and windows before chewing.

Ingredients

1 medium butternut squash (about 2 pounds—large enough to yield 14 ounces uncooked flesh), ends removed

1 cup Fiber One bran cereal (original)

⅓ cup fat-free liquid egg substitute

¼ cup Splenda No Calorie Sweetener (granulated)

1 teaspoon cinnamon

½ teaspoon vanilla extract

⅛ teaspoon salt

½ cup sugar-free pancake syrup

Directions

Preheat oven to 400 degrees.

Place Fiber One in a blender or food processor. Add Splenda, cinnamon, and salt. Grind to a breadcrumb-like consistency, then transfer to a medium bowl.

In a large bowl, combine egg substitute and vanilla extract and stir thoroughly.

Cut squash in half widthwise, making it easier to manage. Peel squash halves using a vegetable peeler or a knife. Cut squash halves in half lengthwise. Scoop out all of the seeds. For exact nutritionals, measure out and use 14 ounces of squash.

Cut squash into French fry shapes. Using paper towels, pat squash pieces firmly to absorb any excess moisture. Spray a baking sheet with nonstick spray.

Toss squash pieces in the egg substitute until they are all evenly covered. One by one, give squash pieces a shake to remove excess egg substitute, coat with breadcrumb mixture, and lay them flat on the sheet.

Bake in the oven for 10 minutes. Carefully flip fries over. Bake in the oven for about 10 additional minutes, or until outsides are crispy and squash is tender. Cooking time will vary depending on how thick your fries are. Serve with pancake syrup for dipping. MMMMMMM!!!!!!!

MAKES 3 SERVINGS

For a pic of this recipe, see the second photo insert. Yay!

Chew on This

In Australia, butternut squash is called "butternut pumpkin" and is used just like ordinary pumpkin. Bet they have some crazy, narrow-headed jack-o'-lanterns down under!

For Weight Watchers *POINTS*®
values and photos of all the
recipes in this book, check out
hungry-girl.com/book.

too-good-to-deny pumpkin pie

PER SERVING (⅛ᵗʰ of pie): 133 calories, 3g fat, 236mg sodium, 28g carbs, 9g fiber, 8g sugars, 6g protein

This is an HG classic. It's our most popular pie recipe of all time—and with good reason. It's SCARY-fantastic!

Ingredients

For Crust

2 cups Fiber One bran cereal (original)

¼ cup light whipped butter or light buttery spread

3 tablespoons Splenda No Calorie Sweetener (granulated)

1 teaspoon cinnamon

For Filling

One 15-ounce can pure pumpkin

One 12-ounce can fat-free evaporated milk

¾ cup Splenda No Calorie Sweetener (granulated)

½ cup fat-free liquid egg substitute

¼ cup sugar-free pancake syrup

1 tablespoon pumpkin pie spice

½ teaspoon cinnamon

⅛ teaspoon salt

Optional Topping

Fat Free Reddi-wip

Directions

Preheat oven to 350 degrees.

In a small microwave-safe bowl, combine butter with 2 tablespoons water. Microwave until just melted.

In a blender or food processor, grind Fiber One to a breadcrumb-like consistency.

In a medium mixing bowl, combine butter mixture and crumbs with the Splenda and cinnamon for the crust. Stir until mixed well.

Spray an oven-safe 9-inch pie dish lightly with nonstick spray. Evenly distribute crust mixture, using your hands or a flat utensil to firmly press and form the crust. Press crust mixture into the edges and up along the sides of the dish, then set aside.

In a large mixing bowl, combine all of the ingredients for the filling. Mix well and pour into pie crust. The filling may be taller than the crust—trust us, this is okay!

Bake pie in the oven for 45 minutes, or until the center is set.

Allow pie to cool slightly. Refrigerate for several hours minimum (overnight is best). Keep refrigerated until ready to serve. Cut into eight slices and, if you like, top with Reddi-wip before serving!!

MAKES 8 SERVINGS

HG Fiber Fact!

The Hungry Girl subscribers have spoken. A 2008 poll found that HGers love Fiber One Chewy Bars more than other leading cereal bars. Each Fiber One Chewy Bar has 9 grams fiber (and they taste like candy!).

fiber-ific fried cheese sticks

PER SERVING (4 pieces): 155 calories, 5.5g fat, 500mg sodium, 13.5g carbs, 7g fiber, 0g sugars, 19g protein

Mozzarella sticks are no longer just bar food, friends. Fiber One + low-fat cheese sticks = GENIUS!

Ingredients

2 pieces light mozzarella string cheese
¼ cup Fiber One bran cereal (original)
2 tablespoons fat-free liquid egg substitute
Salt, black pepper, and Italian seasonings, to taste
Optional dip: low-fat marinara sauce

Directions

Preheat oven to 375 degrees.

In a food processor or blender, grind Fiber One to a breadcrumb-like consistency. Place crumbs in a sealable plastic bag or a container with a lid. Season crumbs with as much salt, pepper, and Italian seasonings as you like. Set aside.

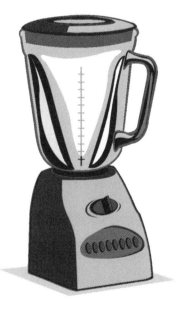

Cut both pieces of string cheese in half so that you have four short sticks. Place sticks in a small bowl and cover them with egg substitute. Swirl egg substitute around so that it thoroughly coats the cheese sticks. One by one, give sticks a shake to remove excess egg substitute and transfer them to the container/bag with the crumbs.

Seal bag or cover container and shake well, coating the sticks completely with the crumbs. Carefully return sticks to the dish with the egg substitute and coat them again. Return cheese sticks to the crumbs, seal or cover, and shake once more to coat.

Place sticks in a baking dish sprayed lightly with nonstick spray. Spritz the tops of the sticks with a quick mist of spray.

Bake for 10 minutes, or until the first sign of cheese oozing out. Serve with warm marinara sauce, if you like. These are best when eaten almost immediately, while the cheese is still hot and gooey!

MAKES 1 SERVING

HG Trivia Tidbit:

Are you sitting down? A large order of mozzarella sticks at Arby's has 849 calories and 56 grams fat! AHHHHHH!

For Weight Watchers **POINTS**®
values and photos of all the
recipes in this book, check out
hungry-girl.com/book.

bloomin' blossom

PER SERVING (½ of recipe with sauce): 192 calories, 1.75g fat, 700mg sodium, 54g carbs, 17g fiber, 13g sugars, 7g protein

Skip the ginormous deep-fried onion disasters at chain restaurants. Really. Skip 'em. They're just CRAZY. The Bloomin' Blossom is a reasonable and delicious fiber-packed swap.

Ingredients

For Onion
1 jumbo sweet onion, not peeled
1 cup Fiber One bran cereal (original)
½ cup fat-free liquid egg substitute
¼ teaspoon seasoned salt
¼ teaspoon garlic powder
⅛ teaspoon black pepper

For Sauce
3 tablespoons fat-free mayonnaise
2 teaspoons ketchup
⅛ teaspoon seasoned salt
Dash chili powder

Directions

Preheat oven to 400 degrees.

In a small bowl, combine all of the ingredients for the sauce. Mix well and refrigerate until ready to serve.

Place Fiber One in a blender or food processor with seasoned salt, garlic powder, and pepper. Grind to a breadcrumb-like consistency and set aside.

Cut the top ½-inch of the onion off (from the pointy side, not the flat one). Leaving the root at the bottom intact, carefully peel off the outside layer.

Starting from the top, carefully cut the onion down the middle, stopping about ½-inch from the root. Repeat to make a crisscross, cutting the onion down the middle again and stopping ½-inch from the bottom. You should now have four sections still attached at the bottom.

Cut each of the four sections down the middle from the top, again stopping before you get to the root.

Place onion, cut side up, in a large bowl and cover completely with ice water. Allow to sit for 5 to 10 minutes, until "petals" open up. Use your hands to gently help pry them open once they've been soaking for several minutes.

Drain water and dry both the onion and the bowl. Place the onion back in the bowl with the petals facing up. Pour the egg substitute evenly over the onion, making sure to get in between all the petals—use your hands to separate them. Swirl egg substitute around so the bottom and sides of the onion get coated.

Flip onion over to drain excess egg substitute. The entire surface of the onion should be covered lightly with egg substitute. Transfer onion to a separate dry bowl.

Slowly sprinkle ground cereal mixture evenly over the onion, making sure to thoroughly coat each petal—use your hands to separate them. Flip the onion upside-down once you're almost done coating it, so that the entire surface gets coated in crumbs. If needed, spread a little more egg substitute on any dry spots to get the crumbs to stick.

Spray a baking dish with nonstick spray and place the onion in it with the petals facing up. Bake in the oven for about 40 minutes, until outside is crispy and inside is soft. Carefully cut out the center of the onion, if you like, so petals are easy to remove. Serve with sauce on the side.

MAKES 2 SERVINGS

Chew on This

We'd like to take a moment to remember the crazy-fatty (and now nonexistent) appetizer known as the Awesome Blossom. The Awesome B was born at Chili's and is survived by its cousins, Bloomin' Onion of Outback Steakhouse and Bloomin' Blossom of Hungry Girl. We'd like to think we helped run it out of town . . .

fiber-fried green beans with spicy cucumber-ranch dip

PER SERVING (½ of recipe with dip): 129 calories, 1.5g fat, 881mg sodium, 32.5g carbs, 14g fiber, 5g sugars, 7g protein

Right after we developed our guilt-free version of this T.G.I. Friday's classic, rumors started swirling that the chain planned to yank theirs from the menu. Coincidence? Perhaps... but we'll never know.

Ingredients

For Green Beans

2 cups (8 ounces) fresh green beans, trimmed

¾ cup Fiber One bran cereal (original)

¼ cup fat-free liquid egg substitute

½ teaspoon onion powder

½ teaspoon garlic powder

¼ teaspoon salt

⅛ teaspoon black pepper

For Dip

3 tablespoons fat-free mayonnaise

2 tablespoons peeled and chopped cucumber

1 tablespoon fat-free sour cream

1½ teaspoons dry ranch dressing/dip mix

¼ teaspoon wasabi paste

Dash cayenne pepper

Directions

Preheat oven to 400 degrees.

Combine all of the ingredients for dip in a food processor or small blender (the Magic Bullet works wonders!). Blend until smooth. Place dip in a small dish and refrigerate until ready to serve.

Place green beans in a large pot with 4 cups water. Bring to a boil. Once boiling, cook for 9 minutes.

Carefully drain green beans. Place them in cold water for a few minutes to stop the cooking process. Drain and dry them well.

Place Fiber One in a blender or food processor. Add onion powder, garlic powder, salt, and black pepper. Add extra seasonings, if you like. Grind to a breadcrumb-like consistency and set aside.

Cover a large baking sheet with aluminum foil and/or spray with nonstick spray. Place egg substitute in a small bowl.

Place about one-third of the crumbs in a large sealable plastic bag. One by one, dip green beans into the egg substitute, give them a shake to remove excess egg substitute, and place them in the bag with the breadcrumbs—continue this with one-third of the beans. Seal the bag and shake it up. Remove the "breaded" green beans and place them on the baking sheet.

Repeat the above step twice more, so that all of the green beans are coated.

Bake in the oven for about 16 minutes, carefully flipping green beans halfway through cooking. Beans are done once they're crispy. Serve with dip and enjoy!

MAKES 2 SERVINGS

Chew on This

In France, green beans are called *haricots verts*. It's basically an exact translation. *Haricot* means "bean" and *vert* means "green." Fancy!

key lime mousse pie

PER SERVING (⅛th of pie): 88 calories, 3g fat, 129mg sodium, 17.5g carbs, 6g fiber, 2g sugars, 1g protein

Fluffy, puffy, and pie-y! This one is sure to please lime-lovers everywhere. Don't like lime much? Move right on ...

Ingredients

For Crust

1¾ cups Fiber One bran cereal (original)

¼ cup light whipped butter or light buttery spread

4 no-calorie sweetener packets

1 teaspoon cinnamon

For Filling

1 small (4-serving) package (or half an 8-serving package) Jell-O Sugar Free Lime Gelatin Dessert Mix

2 cups Cool Whip Free, thawed

1½ tablespoons lemon juice

¼ teaspoon vanilla extract

1 no-calorie sweetener packet

Directions

Preheat oven to 350 degrees.

In a small microwave-safe bowl, combine butter with 2 tablespoons water. Microwave until just melted.

In a blender or food processor, grind Fiber One to a breadcrumb-like consistency.

In a medium mixing bowl, combine Fiber One crumbs and butter mixture with remaining ingredients for crust. Stir until mixed well.

Spray an oven-safe 9-inch pie dish lightly with nonstick spray. Evenly distribute crust mixture in the dish, using your hands or a flat utensil to firmly press and form the crust. Press it into the edges and up along the sides of the dish.

Bake crust in the oven for 10 minutes and then allow to cool.

Meanwhile, in a medium mixing bowl, combine 1 cup boiling water with gelatin mix and sweetener. Stir for at least 2 minutes, until completely dissolved. Add ½ cup cold water, lemon juice, and vanilla extract, and mix well. Refrigerate for about 45 minutes, until slightly thickened but not set.

Once gelatin has thickened slightly, stir in the Cool Whip. Whisk until thoroughly blended, then pour mixture into the pie crust.

Refrigerate until firm, at least 2 hours. Store in the refrigerator until ready to serve. Cut into eight slices and enjoy!

MAKES 8 SERVINGS

HG Fast Fact:

Unlike regular limes, key limes aren't ripe until the peel turns yellow. That part's *key* . . .

fluffy lemon squares

Light 'n lemony, these squares are actually refreshing. Unlike traditional lemon bars, ours won't weigh you down or use up an entire meal's worth of calories. Yippee!

Ingredients

For Crust

1½ cups Fiber One bran cereal (original)

¼ cup light whipped butter or light buttery spread

4 no-calorie sweetener packets

For Filling

1 cup fat-free liquid egg substitute

1⅔ cups Splenda No Calorie Sweetener (granulated)

⅓ cup granulated white sugar

6 tablespoons whole-wheat flour

6 tablespoons freshly squeezed lemon juice (about 2 to 3 lemons' worth)

2 tablespoons lemon zest

2 teaspoons baking powder

Directions

Preheat oven to 350 degrees.

In a small microwave-safe bowl, combine butter with 2 tablespoons water. Microwave until just melted.

In a blender or food processor, grind Fiber One to a breadcrumb-like consistency.

In a medium mixing bowl, combine crumbs, butter mixture, and the contents of the sweetener packets. Stir until mixed well.

Spray a medium oven-safe dish (8-inch by 8-inch works well) lightly with nonstick spray. Evenly distribute crust mixture, using your hands or a flat utensil to firmly press and form the crust. Press it into the edges of the dish. Bake crust in the oven for 5 minutes, then set aside.

In a large mixing bowl, combine egg substitute, Splenda, sugar, flour, lemon juice, lemon zest, and baking powder until mixed well. Pour the filling mixture into the crust.

Bake in the oven for about 20 minutes, until a toothpick inserted into the center comes out clean. Let cool and cut into nine squares.

MAKES 9 SERVINGS

HG Tip! Before grating the zest from your lemons, wash them and remove those pesky produce stickers.

Unexpected Fiber Alert!
Fiber-packed yogurt? Fiber One Creamy Nonfat Yogurt crams 5 grams of the stuff into every 4-ounce container. And it tastes great, too. Weeeeee!

san diego baja-style fish tacos

PER SERVING (1 taco with sauce): 152 calories, 2g fat, 499mg sodium, 23.5g carbs, 5.5g fiber, 3.5g sugars, 14g protein

Here's yet another clever way to use Fiber One for faux-frying. These tacos are very filling (you get a nice hunk of fish in each one)!

Ingredients

HG Heads Up!
If you don't have a broiler pan for your oven, just follow the toaster oven directions. If you don't have a toaster oven . . . borrow one!

For Tacos
4 small white corn tortillas
8 ounces raw cod, cut into 4 even strips
1 cup thinly sliced green cabbage
½ cup Fiber One bran cereal (original)
¼ cup fat-free liquid egg substitute
1 tablespoon seasoned rice vinegar
¼ teaspoon garlic salt
⅛ teaspoon onion powder
⅛ teaspoon garlic powder
Salt, black pepper, additional seasonings, to taste
Optional: chopped cilantro, lime wedges, salsa

For Sauce
⅓ cup fat-free mayonnaise
2 tablespoons fat-free sour cream
2 tablespoons chopped sweet or yellow onion
½ teaspoon lime juice
Dash salt
Dash cayenne

Directions

If using a toaster oven, spray the rack with nonstick spray and line the bottom with aluminum foil. Then preheat toaster oven to 450 degrees.

If using a broiler pan, preheat oven to 450 degrees. Then line the bottom of the broiler pan with aluminum foil and spray the pan's rack with nonstick spray.

In a small bowl, combine all of the ingredients for the sauce and mix well. Refrigerate until ready to assemble tacos.

In another small bowl, toss cabbage with vinegar until lightly coated. Refrigerate until ready to assemble tacos.

In a blender or food processor, grind Fiber One cereal to a breadcrumb-like consistency. Place crumbs in a medium bowl. Mix in garlic salt, onion powder, and garlic powder. Add as much salt and pepper as you like. Feel free to season crumbs with extra spices, as well.

Place egg substitute in another medium bowl. One by one, coat fish strips in egg substitute, give them a shake to remove excess egg substitute, then coat with breadcrumb mixture.

Spray the tops of the breaded fish strips with a light mist of nonstick spray. Place them on the rack of either the toaster oven or the broiler pan. If using the broiler pan, place it in the oven. Cook for 12 minutes, or until the fish is flaky and the tops are brown and crispy.

To assemble tacos, warm tortillas in the microwave for 5 to 10 seconds. Set one fish strip in the middle of each tortilla. Top each piece of fish with one-fourth of the cabbage followed by one-fourth of the sauce. Serve with cilantro, lime wedges, and/or salsa, if you like. Chew!

MAKES 4 SERVINGS

sweet crust quiche supreme

Spinach, bacon, mushrooms, and cheese living together inside one sweet-crusted quiche? Yum!!!

Ingredients

For Crust
1¾ cups Fiber One bran cereal (original)
¼ cup light whipped butter or light buttery spread
4 no-calorie sweetener packets
1 teaspoon cinnamon

For Filling
One 10-ounce package frozen chopped spinach, thawed
4 slices extra-lean turkey bacon
1½ cups fat-free liquid egg substitute
½ cup chopped mushrooms
¼ cup shredded fat-free cheddar cheese
¼ cup fat-free half & half
½ teaspoon baking powder
¼ teaspoon salt

Directions

Preheat oven to 350 degrees.

In a blender or food processor, grind Fiber One to a breadcrumb-like consistency.

Melt butter and mix with 2 tablespoons water. In a medium mixing bowl, combine butter mixture and crumbs with remaining ingredients for crust. Stir until mixed well.

Spray an oven-safe 9-inch pie dish lightly with nonstick spray. Evenly distribute crumb mixture in the dish, using your hands or a flat utensil to firmly press and form crust. Press it into the edges and up along the sides of the dish.

Bake crust in the oven for 10 minutes. Remove and allow to cool. Leave oven on.

Over medium heat, cook bacon in a pan sprayed with nonstick spray on the stove until both sides are crispy. Once cool enough to handle, cut into small, bite-sized pieces.

In a large mixing bowl, combine bacon with all of the other filling ingredients and stir well.

Pour filling mixture into crust. Bake in the oven for 35 minutes, until center is set. Let cool before cutting. Cut into six slices and enjoy!

MAKES 6 SERVINGS

For Weight Watchers **POINTS**®
values and photos of all the
recipes in this book, check out
hungry-girl.com/book.

no-harm eggplant parm

By now, you know that Fiber One crumbs can do magical things in the kitchen.
Here's a completely guilt-free eggplant Parmesan recipe ...

Ingredients

1 large eggplant, ends removed

1 cup Fiber One bran cereal (original)

1 cup canned tomato sauce with Italian seasonings

1 cup shredded fat-free mozzarella cheese

½ cup fat-free liquid egg substitute

¼ cup reduced-fat Parmesan-style grated topping

½ teaspoon garlic powder

⅛ teaspoon salt

⅛ teaspoon black pepper

Optional: dried Italian seasonings (basil, oregano, etc.)

Directions

Preheat oven to 375 degrees.

In a blender or food processor, grind Fiber One to a breadcrumb-like consistency. Add garlic powder, salt, and pepper. Season to taste with optional seasonings, if you like. Transfer to a medium bowl and set aside.

Pour egg substitute into a separate medium bowl and set that aside as well.

Cut eggplant lengthwise into ½-inch slices. Use paper towels to blot eggplant slices on both sides, removing excess moisture.

Spray a large baking pan with nonstick spray.

Coat eggplant slices on both sides—first with egg substitute, and then with crumb mixture. Arrange slices flat in the baking pan and bake in the oven for 30 minutes.

Flip slices over and bake until browned on both sides, about 10 minutes longer. Remove pan from oven, but leave oven on.

Spray an 8-inch by 8-inch baking dish lightly with nonstick spray. Spread ¼ cup sauce in the bottom. Arrange half the baked eggplant slices evenly over the sauce.

Continue to layer ingredients evenly in this order: sauce (¼ cup), mozzarella and Parm-style topping (half of each), sauce (¼ cup), eggplant (remaining slices), sauce (¼ cup), and cheeses (remaining amounts).

Cover dish with foil and return to the oven. Bake for 25 minutes, or until heated through. Allow to cool slightly, and then cut into quarters. Devour!

MAKES 4 SERVINGS

HG Fast Fact:

The eggplant-colored crayon was added to Crayola's crayon lineup in 1998. You can find it in the box of 120 colors and, according to the Crayola website, Eggplant is ranked number 81 overall. This recipe for No-Harm Eggplant Parm is WAY more popular.

vanilla crème pumpkin cheesecake

PER SERVING (1/12th of cake with topping): 160 calories, 3.25g fat, 579mg sodium, 20g carbs, 5g fiber, 7g sugars, 15g protein

You want a large-and-in-charge, twelve-serving, guilt-free pumpkin cheesecake? Here it is!

Ingredients

For Crust
2 cups Fiber One bran cereal (original)
¼ cup light whipped butter or light buttery spread
3 tablespoons Splenda No Calorie Sweetener (granulated)
1 teaspoon cinnamon

For Filling
32 ounces fat-free cream cheese, room temperature
1 cup fat-free liquid egg substitute
1 cup canned pure pumpkin
1 cup Splenda No Calorie Sweetener (granulated)
¼ cup light brown sugar (not packed)
1 teaspoon vanilla extract
1 teaspoon pumpkin pie spice

For Topping
¾ cup fat-free sour cream
¼ cup Splenda No Calorie Sweetener (granulated)
½ teaspoon vanilla extract

Directions

Preheat oven to 325 degrees.

In a blender or food processor, grind Fiber One to a breadcrumb-like consistency. Transfer to a medium bowl and set aside.

Melt butter and mix with 2 tablespoons water. Add butter mixture and other crust ingredients to cereal crumbs and mix thoroughly.

Spray a nonstick springform pie pan (about 9 inches wide) lightly with nonstick spray—make sure to get the sides as well as the bottom. Evenly distribute crumb mixture, using your hands or a flat utensil to firmly press and form the crust along the bottom of the pan. Set aside.

In a large mixing bowl, combine all of the filling ingredients. Using an electric mixer set to medium speed, mix until completely blended and lump-free. Pour mixture into the pan.

Bake in the oven for approximately 1 hour and 20 minutes, until set. Allow cake to chill in the fridge for at least 3 to 4 hours (overnight is best).

Once cake has chilled, carefully release and remove springform top. In a small dish, combine all topping ingredients. Mix well and spread evenly over the cake.

Return cake to the fridge until topping has chilled and set, or until ready to serve. Cut into twelve slices and enjoy!

MAKES 12 SERVINGS

HG Tip! Save time . . . make this cake the night before a party. Then just do the topping the day of!

HG Fast Fact:

A slice of pumpkin cheesecake from a restaurant packs in around 400 calories and 26 grams fat. You could eat HALF of ours and still not come close to taking in that much fat. Cheesecake can be SCARY!

s'mores krispymallow treats

PER SERVING (1 square): 57 calories, 1g fat, 52mg sodium, 12g carbs, 1.5g fiber, 5g sugars, 0.5g protein

Just when you thought Krispymallow Treats (see the first HG book for those) couldn't get any better ... here's a S'MORES version. Exciting!!!

Ingredients

4 cups puffed wheat cereal
2 cups Golden Grahams cereal
1 cup Fiber One bran cereal (original)
3 cups mini marshmallows
3 tablespoons light whipped butter or light buttery spread
5 teaspoons mini semi-sweet chocolate chips

Directions

Melt butter in a large saucepan over low heat. Add marshmallows and stir until completely melted, then remove from heat. Add all three cereals and stir until thoroughly coated.

Spray a 9-inch by 13-inch baking pan with nonstick spray. Using a spatula, press marshmallow-cereal mixture evenly into the pan. Allow to cool.

Sprinkle mini chocolate chips evenly over the top of the pan. Press down on the contents of the pan with a spatula. Cut into twenty-five squares. Enjoy your treat!

MAKES 25 SERVINGS

HG Trivia Tidbit:

The original Rice Krispies Treats were invented in 1939 by Mary Barber and the Kellogg's Home Economics Department. The original s'mores were inspired by Girl Scouts in the 1920s. And in 2008, when Hungry Girl put the two together, history (and an insanely good snack!) was made.

TOP ATE Tips for Faux-Frying

1. Grind up a big batch of Fiber One all at once. Stash it in an airtight container, and you'll get to skip the "grind to a breadcrumb-like consistency" step the next time you faux-fry. FYI, a quarter cup of the crumbs is equal to a half cup of the cereal.

2. Raid your spice rack. Get crazy and add your favorite seasonings (cayenne pepper, taco seasoning mix, dried basil, etc.) to your crumbs. High fiber *and* high flavor . . .

3. Swap out the egg substitute. The egg is only there to help the crumbs stick to your food. So if there's a guilt-free sauce or dressing you love, coat your food in that before you roll it in Fiber One crumbs for an extra flavor boost.

4. Have extra ingredients on hand. Our recipes call for pretty much the exact amount of Fiber One and egg substitute needed to coat your food completely, which means you may feel like you're running out at the end. To avoid any stress, portion out a little more than what's called for.

5. Insist on the one-and-only Fiber One bran cereal (original). Do not, under any circumstances, attempt to faux-fry with some other high-fiber cereal, including the other varieties of F1. Caramel Delight onion rings = not recommended.

6. Mix 'n match. Can't decide between Faux-Fried Zucchini and Fiber-ific Fried Cheese Sticks? No problem! Grab whatever you have in the fridge (within reason), roll it all in crumbly goodness, and serve it up with a couple yummy dipping sauces. It'll be like having one of those restaurant sampler platters, without all the grease.

7. Eyes bigger than your stomach? There's no shame in leftovers, but your faux-fried goodies DO typically taste better right out of the oven. If you need to reheat 'em the next day, skip the microwave and pop them in the oven at a high temperature to crisp up. Just make sure they don't burn.

8. Don't stop at these recipes! Use them as jumping-off points and get creative. What else can you roll in fiber-ific breadcrumbs? Mushrooms? Pineapple? Broccoli? Go for it!

chapter fourteen

fun with vitalicious

Muffin-tastic
Fiber-Packed Creations

Anyone who knows anything about Hungry Girl is familiar with the 100-calorie, high-fiber, all-natural, vitamin-packed muffin and brownie treats from Vitalicious. You can find them at select supermarkets, but to get the full selection of flavors, order them from vitalicious.com. A little inconvenient? Perhaps, but they can be stored in the freezer for months and thawed in seconds. Besides, they are SO worth the extra effort. Here are a bunch of recipes featuring these sweet and decadent cake replacements.

dynamite double chocolate dream parfaits

PER SERVING (1 parfait): 165 calories, 2.75g fat, 335mg sodium, 39g carbs, 6.5g fiber, 12g sugars, 4.5g protein

Here's an old HG favorite. It combines vanilla pudding, chocolate pudding, whipped cream, and VitaTops. How could it NOT be fantastic?

Ingredients

2 Double Chocolate Dream VitaTops, thawed
1 Jell-O Sugar Free Vanilla Pudding Snack
1 Jell-O Sugar Free Chocolate Pudding Snack
4 tablespoons Fat Free Reddi-wip

Directions

Break VitaTops up into small pieces. Take one-third of the Vita pieces and distribute between two parfait glasses.

Spoon half of the chocolate pudding into each glass. Take half of the remaining Vita pieces and distribute between the two glasses.

Spoon half of the vanilla pudding into each glass. Top parfaits evenly with the remaining Vita pieces. Finish off with Reddi-wip and enjoy!

MAKES 2 SERVINGS

freezy-cool whoopie pie

PER SERVING (entire dessert): 115 calories, 1.5g fat,
145mg sodium, 24g carbs, 6g fiber, 10g sugars, 3g protein

Whoopie Pie is a New England favorite consisting of a chocolate cake sandwich
filled with creamy goodness. Our version uses two simple ingredients.
So grab a VitaTop and start slicing . . .

Ingredients

1 Deep Chocolate VitaTop, thawed
2 tablespoons Cool Whip Free, thawed

Directions

Carefully slice VitaTop in half
lengthwise, so that you are left
with two thin round Vita "slices."

Spread Cool Whip on one slice and
top with the other slice. Cover with
plastic wrap and freeze until solid,
about 1 hour. Enjoy!

MAKES 1 SERVING

Chew on This

In some parts of the world, whoopie pies are called "gobs." As long as there's a *gob* of
Cool Whip Free between these Vita slices, we'll be screaming "Whoopie!" all day long.

puddin'-packed caramel brownie blitz!

PER SERVING (entire dessert): 154 calories, 2.5g fat,
236mg sodium, 35g carbs, 6g fiber, 11.5g sugars, 4.5g protein

*The word "blitz" is German for "lightning" or "very fast." As in,
once you make this gooey fudge-fest of a dessert, you'll
want to gobble it down lightning fast!*

Ingredients

1 VitaBrownie, thawed
One-half Jell-O Sugar Free Vanilla Pudding Snack
1 teaspoon fat-free caramel dip, room temperature
2 tablespoons Fat Free Reddi-wip

Directions

Microwave brownie until just slightly warm. Slice it in half horizontally, so you have a top piece and a bottom piece.

Spoon pudding over the bottom brownie piece and cover with the top brownie piece. Drizzle caramel over brownie. Cover with Reddi-wip and enjoy!

MAKES 1 SERVING

bananaberry pudding cream pie explosion

PER SERVING (entire dessert): 164 calories, 3g fat, 244mg sodium, 39.5g carbs, 5.25g fiber, 2.5g sugars, 5.5g protein

This little sweet treat combines a lot of flavors you probably love—bananas, walnuts, strawberry, and vanilla. Mmmmmm . . .

Ingredients

1 Sugar Free Banana Nut VitaTop, thawed

One-half Jell-O Sugar Free Vanilla Pudding Snack

2 tablespoons Cool Whip Free, thawed

1 tablespoon sugar-free strawberry preserves

1 strawberry, sliced

¼ sheet (1 cracker) low-fat cinnamon graham crackers, crushed

Directions

Carefully slice VitaTop in half lengthwise, so that you are left with two thin round Vita "slices."

Place the bottom slice on a plate, cut side up, and top with preserves. Spread half of the pudding (one-fourth of the Pudding Snack) on top.

Place top Vita slice over pudding layer, cut side down. Cover with remaining pudding (another fourth of the Pudding Snack).

Top with strawberry slices and cover with Cool Whip. Sprinkle dessert with crushed graham crackers. Mmmm!

MAKES 1 SERVING

For Weight Watchers *POINTS*® values and photos of all the recipes in this book, check out hungry-girl.com/book.

mile-high choco-berry vitatop pie

PER SERVING (½ of pie): 145 calories, 2.25g fat, 155mg sodium, 33g carbs, 5.5g fiber, 13g sugars, 3g protein

This dessert isn't REALLY a mile high, but it is very tall. So tall, in fact, that it may topple over if you're not super-careful. So be super-careful!

Ingredients

2 VitaTops (any chocolate flavor), thawed

¼ cup plus 2 tablespoons Cool Whip Free, thawed, divided

2 tablespoons sugar-free strawberry preserves

1 teaspoon mini semi-sweet chocolate chips

Directions

In a small bowl, combine ¼ cup Cool Whip with preserves. Stir until blended and set aside.

Carefully slice VitaTops in half lengthwise, so that you are left with four thin round "slices." The two slices from the tops of the Vitas will be the top and bottom of your pie. Place one of those top pieces on a plate, cut side up, and set the other aside to be used last.

Spread half of the Cool Whip–preserves mixture over the Vita slice on the plate. Place another Vita slice on top.

Spread 1 tablespoon Cool Whip over that slice. Top with a third Vita slice. Cover with remaining Cool Whip–preserves mixture and top with your final Vita slice, cut side down.

Spread 1 tablespoon Cool Whip on top. Sprinkle with mini chocolate chips. Freeze until solid, about 1 hour. Cut pie down the center and share with a pal!

MAKES 2 SERVINGS

Chew on This

Denver, Colorado, is known as the Mile-High City because it's exactly a mile above sea level. Our pie is known as "mile-high" because it's kinda tall.

chocolate fluff 'n nutter

PER SERVING (entire dessert): 176 calories, 4.5g fat,
211mg sodium, 32.5g carbs, 6.5g fiber, 16.5g sugars, 5g protein

It's a modern HG twist on your old favorite.
Fluffy marshmallow + peanut butter = happiness.

Ingredients

1 Fudgy Peanut Butter Chip VitaTop, slightly thawed
1 tablespoon Jet-Puffed Marshmallow Creme
1 tablespoon Cool Whip Free, thawed
½ tablespoon reduced-fat peanut butter

Directions

Carefully slice VitaTop in half lengthwise, so that you are left with two thin round Vita "slices."

Wrap Vita slices in a paper towel. Microwave for 10 to 20 seconds, until peanut butter chips have melted slightly. Let cool.

In a small bowl, combine Cool Whip and peanut butter. Mix well and set aside.

Place bottom Vita slice on a plate, cut side up. Spread Cool Whip–peanut butter mixture evenly on top.

Place the top Vita slice over the Cool Whip–peanut butter mixture, cut side down. Spread marshmallow creme on top of that, making sure to mix with some of the peanut buttery goodness from the melted chips. Eat immediately.

MAKES 1 SERVING

black forest cheesecake parfait

PER SERVING (entire parfait): 144 calories, 1.75g fat,
252mg sodium, 30g carbs, 5.25g fiber, 14.5g sugars, 5.5g protein

Never underestimate the power of a VitaTop. Even one that's broken into small pieces.

Ingredients

1 Triple Chocolate Chunk VitaTop, thawed
2 tablespoons canned cherries packed in water, drained
1 tablespoon fat-free cream cheese, room temperature
¼ teaspoon Coffee-mate Sugar Free French Vanilla powdered creamer
2 no-calorie sweetener packets
2 tablespoons Fat Free Reddi-wip

Directions

In a small bowl, combine powdered creamer with contents of 1 sweetener packet and 2 tablespoons hot water. Mix well to dissolve. Stir in cream cheese until thoroughly blended. Set aside.

In a separate small bowl, combine cherries with 1 teaspoon water and contents of the other sweetener packet. Mix well.

Cut VitaTop into small pieces. Place half of the pieces in a parfait glass. Cover with half of the cherry mixture, then top with half of the cream cheese mixture.

Add the remaining Vita pieces to the parfait glass. Top with remaining cream cheese mixture. Finish off with the rest of the cherry mixture. Top with Reddi-wip and dig in!

MAKES 1 SERVING

For Weight Watchers *POINTS*® values and photos of all the recipes in this book, check out hungry-girl.com/book.

yogurt-smothered apple 'n apricot surprise

PER SERVING (entire recipe): 165 calories, 1g fat, 185mg sodium, 38g carbs, 6g fiber, 15.5g sugars, 6g protein

Looking for a brand-new, creative, super-easy and completely DELICIOUS breakfast? Here it is!

◌ Ingredients

1 AppleBerry VitaTop, thawed
3 ounces Yoplait Light Apple Turnover yogurt
1 tablespoon sugar-free apricot preserves

◌ Directions

Place VitaTop on a microwave-safe plate. Microwave for about 20 seconds, until warm.

Spread preserves over VitaTop. Smother with yogurt and enjoy!

MAKES 1 SERVING

chocolate for breakfast vitasundae

PER SERVING (entire sundae): 194 calories, 1.75g fat, 215mg sodium, 42g carbs, 7.5g fiber, 26.5g sugars, 8g protein

Here's another fantastic breakfast recipe featuring VitaTops. And yes, it's OK to chew chocolate in the A.M. Woohoo!

Ingredients

1 VitaTop (any chocolate flavor), thawed
4 ounces fat-free vanilla yogurt
½ cup chopped strawberries

Directions

Break VitaTop into pieces and place in the blender. Pulse until reduced to crumbs.

Place one-third of the Vita crumbs in a small glass or bowl. Top with one-third of the strawberries. Add half of the yogurt.

Sprinkle half of the remaining Vita crumbs over the yogurt. Top with half of the rest of the strawberries.

Spread the remaining yogurt over the strawberries. Top with the rest of the Vita crumbs. Finish it all off with remaining strawberries and eat up! Yes!

MAKES 1 SERVING

double-trouble chocolate trifle

PER SERVING (¼ᵗʰ of trifle): 193 calories, 1.5g fat, 346mg sodium, 39.5g carbs, 6.5g fiber, 15g sugars, 5.5g protein

Holy cow! This dessert is so good that mere words cannot do it justice. It's the type of trouble everyone will WANT to get into.

Ingredients

4 VitaTops (any chocolate flavor), thawed
1⅔ cups Cool Whip Free, thawed, divided
1 cup skim milk
2 tablespoons sugar-free fat-free chocolate instant pudding mix
1½ tablespoons sugar-free chocolate syrup

Directions

In a mixing bowl, combine skim milk with pudding mix. Whisk until blended and thickened, about 2 minutes. Refrigerate for at least 5 minutes.

In a separate mixing bowl, combine syrup with 1 cup Cool Whip. Mix gently until completely blended. Refrigerate for at least 5 minutes.

Break VitaTops into pieces and place in the blender. Pulse until reduced to crumbs.

In the bottom of a medium serving bowl, layer one-fourth of the Vita crumbs. Top with half of the pudding.

Spread ⅔ cup Cool Whip over pudding layer. Sprinkle evenly with two-thirds of the remaining Vita crumbs.

Spread the remaining pudding in a layer over the Vita crumbs. Top with the chocolate syrup–Cool Whip mixture. Finally, sprinkle remaining Vita crumbs over the top and dig in!

MAKES 4 SERVINGS

 For a pic of this recipe, see the second photo insert. Yay!

HG Fast Fact:

The word "trifle" can mean "of little importance or value." That DEFINITELY does not apply to this particular trifle, which can and should be a super-important and valuable part of your life.

HG's Top Secret Food Finds!

Vitalicious products aren't the only little-known food finds on HG's list of favorites. Here are some of our other underground picks. These are worth seeking out!

* **Vivi's Original Sauce, Classic Carnival Mustard:**

   The world's BEST condiment. It's great with everything from hot dogs to tuna. Spread it on sandwiches, cook with it, or use it as a dip.

   vivisoriginalsauce.com

* **Justin's Nut Butter 100 Calorie Squeeze Packs:**

   Portion-controlled peanut butter is worth the trouble. Order these cute packets in Honey Peanut Butter Blend and Maple Almond Butter.

   justinsnutbutter.com

* **Western Bagel Alternative Bagels:**

   These high-fiber, low-calorie bagels come in a slew of flavors and they're all fantastic. Each one has 110 calories and 7 to 8 grams of fiber.

   westernbagel.com

* **Hoffy Extra Lean Beef Franks, Quarter Pounder Big Dog:**

   WOW! These dogs are ginormously delicious and clock in with only 110 calories and 5 grams of fat. (Pssst . . . our pals at *heavenlydietstore.com* ship these out nationwide in the winter.)

   squarehbrands.com

* **Tasty Eats Soy Jerky, Hot N' Spicy:**

   This stuff does NOT taste like "soy" anything, and it isn't even hot and/or spicy—it's sweet and delicious and only has 45 calories and less than 1 gram of fat per serving.

   tastyeats.com

Whew . . . there you have it. Two hundred insanely fantastic recipes, each with under 200 itty-bitty calories. Hope you enjoy them as much as the entire HG staff and I do. If you want to tell us your favorites, or give us feedback on any of the recipes, please email us at hgbooks@hungry-girl.com. It's always great to hear from you and it makes us all feel popular.

And remember, for more recipes, food finds, tips & tricks, sign up for our free daily emails at Hungry-Girl.com. *HG out!*

HUNGRY2

Index